you and your YORKIE PUPPY

in a nutshell

The essential owners' guide to perfect puppy
parenting – with easy-to-follow steps on how
to choose and care for your new arrival

Carry Aylward

NUTSHELL
BOOKS

Front cover design by Nutshell Books
Book design by Nutshell Books
Photography: © AdobeStock,
© Dreamstime, © iStock

Printed by Kindle Direct Publishing

First printed 2020

Nutshell Books
3 Holmlea Road, Goring on Thames
RG8 9EX, United Kingdom
www.nutshell-books.com

*To you, the reader, for wanting to be a great
Yorkie owner, and for the super-special puppy
you bring into your heart and home*

CONTENTS

FOREWORD

Priceless! That's Yorkshire Terriers for you. On the one hand, they're the glitzy glamorous celebrities of the dog world. And on the other, they're the rough-and-ready rat-catching ruffians of nineteenth-century industry.

Either way, these small but larger-than-life characters – more affectionately known as Yorkies – are utterly priceless. They are little gems to be treasured and cherished. They will brighten your day as they steal your heart.

Needless to say, if you are considering a puppy from this precious breed, I am thrilled for you. And congratulations too on taking this step towards being an excellent owner. Because adorable and delightful as they are, these little toy-terriers can also be anything from demanding and challenging to downright deliberately naughty. So whether or not you've owned one before, you've chosen the perfect starter guide for Yorkie puppy parents-to-be.

This book answers the most important early-stage questions and leads you step by step through the process, from deciding whether a Yorkie is right for you, through the first days to the subsequent weeks and months – that all-important formative time when your puppy is growing and learning at its fastest. And when you need to put the most energy into its upbringing and training.

This guide is intentionally concise, bringing together up-to-date research in an easy-to-read, easy-to-follow format that gives you only what you need to know, when you need to know it.

Also for the sake of easy reading, your puppy is referred to as 'she' from here on, but please consider 'she' to mean 'he or she' in every instance.

The advice that follows will help you to build a solid foundation for a wonderful relationship with your Yorkie. It will keep you smiling through the love and the cuddles as well as the puddles and poops, the heart-wrenching nights and the shredded items of value.

For now, all you need do is brace yourself with unconditional love and an unfaltering sense of humor.

I. YORKIES AND YOU

When you choose the 'Yorkie' way, know that a typical
Yorkie will chase after anything that moves and ward off
the enemy with its piercing bark. And it will do this just
as readily as it will ponce around with its head held
high, in its inimitably self-important manner, before
snuggling up for a snooze on your lap.

Understand that with the silky-smooth cuddles and
bright-eyed devotion, you are also choosing a spirited
and determined companion with often-astounding
attitude.

Don't be taken in by her daintiness and charm; or
fooled by her tenacity and self-confidence. Be ready for
both because these dogs truly are part lapdog, part feisty
terrier. And considering their history it's no surprise.

The breed was developed in the 1880s in the north-
English county of Yorkshire, where their small size and
terrier instincts made them great rat catchers, and they
earned their living hunting vermin in the textile mills
and mines. But with their silken coats and self-important
mannerisms, they quickly became fashionable lapdogs
for well-to-do Victorian ladies, earning their livings
instead as pampered companion dogs.

Be ready for these two distinct sides to the Yorkie.
Expect them and cherish them. Then – whether yours is
sashaying along the sidewalk or being bossy and
belligerent – you'll have the makings of an

understanding, appreciative owner. And as long as your Yorkie is well-raised and well-treated, there's every reason to expect that she will make a wonderful pet for you too.

The Yorkshire Terrier is not the only delightful 'Yorkie'
to hail from Yorkshire. In the UK, the Yorkie chocolate
bar is also a much-loved treat. Both, of course, are
incredibly sweet.

Decisions, decisions!

It could be that a Yorkie puppy is an excellent choice for you, even if you are a first-time dog owner. But before we delve deeper into the characteristics of the breed, let's quickly consider some simple but hugely important questions, because choosing a puppy is a momentous, life-changing and long-term decision.

If you are new to owning a dog – any dog – when you invite one into your world, your life will never be the same. It will be warmer, messier, happier and richer in so many ways. But you will also start thinking differently about what you wear, the places you visit, your vacation destinations and possibly even the car you drive.

So are you really ready for a dog?

If you invite a dog into your home, she should be treated like family. Ask yourself very honestly whether, at this time in your life, and for the next 12-plus years, you will be able to give her the love, care, time, exercise, training and patience she deserves. No dog should ever be cast aside like a pair of shoes its owner has grown tired of.

Is a puppy right for you?

Ask yourself honestly whether you can face the puppy stage with the pooping, weeing and chewing of everything in sight. If not, you might consider taking on an older dog. An adult that needs rehoming will have finished with toilet training, teething and even adolescence.

Another option is to give a home to a dog in its senior years. There are so many beautiful older dogs that need re-homing through no fault of their own, so if you are no longer as strong or active as you once were, this might be the most sensible choice for you now.

Do you have other pets?

If you already have other dogs or cats, consider carefully how a new dog would fit in to your family. If you choose a Yorkie puppy, and socialize it well, there's no reason for her to have a problem with your existing animals. However, those pets might not be quite so adaptable to your new puppy.

You still want a puppy?

I know. They're warm and cuddly and there's nothing as sweet as the pitter patter of puppy feet. But the first steps to getting a puppy are a big investment – not just financially, but also in terms of time, energy and emotion. This is not an effort to put you off getting a dog. It's just really important that you are sure you are able to give your puppy the happy life it deserves and fully understand the commitment you're making. Too many dogs are re-homed and even put down each year because their owners underestimated the responsibility.

And be sure to involve any other members of the household in this decision. It's very important that everyone has bought into the whole idea from the very start. The more say the family has in owning a dog, choosing the breed, and choosing your specific puppy, the more likely they will be to actively engage with and care for it, and the less likely they'll be to shirk their dog-walking, poo-picking responsibilities.

Finally back to Yorkies

So if you're sure you can give your dog the love and attention she needs and deserves, and you're sure a puppy is the way forward, let's look more closely at the specifics of the Yorkshire Terrier.

Yorkies regularly enjoy the top spot as the favorite breed in the Toy Group of dogs. This is the breed's given category according to both the American Kennel Club (AKC) and the Kennel Club (UK). And even in the rankings of All Breeds, they usually hold a place in the top ten. Yes, they are popular dogs, and it's easy to see why. Besides being loving, loyal and deeply devoted to their owners, they are the most adorable, charismatic and entertaining little poppets. They are playful, expressive, regal, brave, feisty, energetic, adventurous. They are a good choice for first-time dog owners ... and the list goes on.

Yorkies can make incredibly good companions. But being an owner still comes with its fair share of challenges, so consider these traits and characteristics carefully. They're not necessarily good or bad in themselves; just more or less right for you and your circumstances.

Small in size

There are lots of advantages to owning a dog from the Toy Group, most notable of which is probably their suitability for apartment living. Yorkies don't need lots of space or even a yard or garden. They also need less food than bigger breeds, which makes them less expensive to take care of.

They are light-weight which makes them easy to scoop into your arms, easy to handle, and especially easy to take out or travel with. They can be toted around in special dog handbags, or taken to the skies with you inside the cabin of certain aircraft.

And as companions they make ideal lapdogs that can comfortably curl up on your lap for a cuddle.

However, their small, fragile builds make them physically vulnerable, to the extent that everyone in the household needs to be gentle when handling them, and constantly watching where they sit and put their feet.

Yorkies also need especially careful supervision around children and bigger dogs. In fact, this combination of delicate structure and feisty terrier temperament means they are not recommended for households with toddlers, or children too small to understand how to treat them.

Big in personality

What Yorkies lack in size they more than make up for in sparkle and character. They are tenacious, brave and sometimes even bossy. They are bursting with bravado and self-importance, and yet they are sociable and affectionate with it. They are always looking for adventure, fun and trouble. It's their enormous personalities that endear them to their owners who (be warned) become utterly besotted.

However, these larger-than-life personalities come hand-in-hand with high energy levels. Yorkies can be excitable, attention-seeking and demanding, and while this can be appealing and endearing, it can also be very trying on your patience.

Regal AND cute

With their small size, alert expressions and constant readiness to play, Yorkies are the very embodiment of cuteness. Add to this their lustrous coats, and the way they flaunt them with their heads held high and self-important air, and you're faced with the perfect, if unusual, combination of glamorous and drop-dead cute.

On the flip side, depending on how you feel about grooming, the Yorkie's gorgeous silken coat can be time-consuming to care for. These little cuties need regular brushing, and bathing too.

Companionable

Although Yorkies can be Terriers by nature – feisty, brave, independent and investigative – they are listed in the Toy Group because they are a small breed that make wonderful companions or lapdogs. They love sleeping on your lap and are utterly adorable when they do. And they don't need a huge amount of exercise which means they also make great travel companions and excellent therapy dogs.

Typical Yorkies are friendly, hugely affectionate and deeply devoted to their owners. But they have a very real need for their owners' love and companionship too and as a result they can be over-protective at times. This means they're not necessarily good with strangers or small children. It also makes them prone to separation anxiety which means they should never be left alone all day.

Playful

Little rays of sunshine, Yorkies get full marks and more for playfulness. Sparkling, inventive and yes, priceless, they are a constant source of amusement. They love learning new tricks and, being both intelligent and keen to please, they make excellent, fun and entertaining students. And if you already have other pets, they would love to play with them too.

Hypoallergenic

No dog breed is totally hypoallergenic, but Yorkies come very close with their human-like hair. They also don't shed much, so all-in-all they are one of the best choices for allergy sufferers.

Watchdogs

Yorkshire Terriers make excellent watchdogs but be warned, they can be yappy with it.

Tricky to house-train

Like many small dogs, Yorkies are more difficult to house-train than the average breed. Luckily, however, toilet training is a relatively short-term project.

Healthy

As long as Yorkies are not extra small (or 'tea cup' sized), they are generally a healthy breed and live on average between 12 and 15 years. They are not prone to weight gain, possibly because they have delicate digestive systems and can be picky eaters, but it's worth noting that they can suffer teeth or gum problems, so their teeth need regular cleaning. They are also not especially tolerant of hot or cold temperatures.

Bottom line

Every Yorkie has its own delightful personality and sometimes less-delightful traits, and we will look at all of these in more detail. But for now, picture this as a worst-case scenario: yours might take a long time to house-train, chew on items of value, be stubborn and naughty, demanding and noisy. She might become over-protective of you and territorial.

But if you can give her the company, love and attention she needs, keep her active and busy with playtime, toys and exercise, you needn't have difficulty with any of these. You will have fun beyond measure. And those little paws will make the deepest footprints in your heart.

2. WHAT IS A 'TRUE' YORKIE?

You've decided you can give a dog the time, care, expense and devotion it needs, and that you want a Yorkie. I'm thrilled for you. There are wonderful, magical, hilarious, sock-nicking, poo-picking, finger-nipping, chin-licking times ahead. And more love than you could ever imagine.

But don't rush off to see the first litter you come across – even if you want no more from your Yorkie than good company. Why? Because it's close to impossible to resist the pleading eyes of a puppy that wants to go home with you. Once those eyes have found your heart, they are most likely stuck there for life.

Better to plan ahead. Start doing your research so you can make a wise and informed choice. If it's a companion pet you're after, you'll be less particular than someone who's looking for a show dog or a dog you might be thinking of using for breeding. The puppies could all grow into lovely dogs, but if you don't want to risk weak strains and traits, it's well worth taking the time to track down a litter that is a credit to the breed.

Here are some things to understand and consider before you begin your search.

Purebreds

Many puppy farmers and backyard breeders mate their dogs with other breeds, and still advertise them as

Yorkies. Although these puppies might grow into lovely dogs, they are unlikely to have the traits of a true Yorkshire Terrier. The pureness of the breeding is up to you, but if you do want a purebred – meaning its parents are of the same breed – it's important that you see the mother and, if it's not possible to meet the father, that you at least see photos or video footage of him.

Pedigrees

If you want a pedigree Yorkshire Terrier – a purebred dog that is also registered with a recognized and reputable club or society such as the Kennel Club – you must choose a puppy from a breeder that has their assurance.

And if you are planning to show your dog or become a registered breeder yourself, you will certainly need to do more research. The section 'Useful Information' at the end of the book has a list of organizations and websites you can refer to.

But what is a 'good' Yorkshire Terrier?

Dogs entered into showing classes are measured against the Breed Standard, a list of ideal attributes specified by the Kennel Club of that country. The following is a general summary of the qualities and features considered desirable in a Yorkie.

Temperament

Full of personality, and even-tempered with it. Sprightly, alert, intelligent, affectionate and tomboyish.

Physical appearance

- **Overall:** Once fully grown she is long-haired with a coat of steel blue (this is the correct term for a silvery grey) and tan. This hangs evenly and reasonably straight down each side of the body from a parting that runs from head to tail. The body is neat and compact, and the head is carried high in a confident, self-important manner.

- **Coat:** This is of prime importance. It is glossy, fine and silky in texture. On the body it is long and straight, but never impedes movement. It is also long on the top of the head and on the muzzle.
- **Coloring:**
  - Puppies are normally black and tan, with an intermingling of black hairs in the tan.
  - Adult coats are steel blue and tan, and the color of the coat is as important as the length, quality and texture. The dark steel blue extends from the back of the head to the root of the tail, becoming a darker blue on the tail itself. This blue never mingles with the tan. The tan hair is dark at the roots, becoming lighter towards the tips. Hair on head, chest and legs is a bright, rich tan. This becomes deeper still at the sides of the head, on the muzzle and at the roots of the ears.
- **Size:**
  - Weight: Not over 7 lbs (3.2kg)
  - Height: Yorkies are notoriously inconsistent in size, and height is not specified in the breed standards. However they generally stand 8-9 inches (20-23cm) at the shoulder.
- **Eyes:** Dark and sparkling with an intelligent expression. Facing directly forwards, and not too prominent. The edge of the eyelids is dark.
- **Ears:** Small, V-shaped and not too far apart. Carried erect and covered with short hair.

- **Nose:** Black
- **Muzzle:** Not too long
- **Teeth:** Ideally set in a perfect scissor bite where the upper incisor teeth closely overlap the lower ones when the mouth is closed. The AKC will also accept a level bite, where the upper and lower incisors meet edge to edge.
- **Body:** Compact and well-proportioned
- **Back:** Short, with a level backline (the same height at the shoulder as at the rump).
- **Legs:** Straight when viewed from the front and behind.
- **Paws:** Round with black nails
- **Tail:** If docked, it should be medium length and carried a little higher than the level of the back. If undocked, it should be as straight as possible, with plenty of hair and carried higher than the level of the back.

Movement

Free with straight leg action and the backline remaining level.

Of course your puppy – or at this stage her parents – needn't tick all these boxes for her to grow into a lovely dog, but it's useful and interesting to know what is expected of a well-bred Yorkie.

3. FINDING THE LITTER

DECIDE WHAT YOU'RE LOOKING FOR

Before you actually go in search of new litters, you might want to sort out some preferences in your own mind.

Boy or girl?

If you already have another dog, it would be sensible to choose a puppy from the opposite sex to avoid jealousy and competition, especially if either or both of them will be left un-neutered.

But honestly, other dogs aside – and if you're not hoping to use him or her for breeding someday – I don't believe there's much in it. Every Yorkie really is his or her own 'person', and health and temperament are far more important considerations. Good training and keeping your puppy in its right place in the 'pack' are much better determining factors in how he or she will turn out and fit into your family.

Neutering, however, **is** a very important consideration. If un-neutered, females will come into heat approximately every six months – which could result in mood swings and aggressiveness towards other females, and there would also be the risk of unwanted pregnancy. Both males and females, but males to a greater extent, can adopt unwanted sexual behaviors like mounting and lifting their legs inside the house to mark their territory. Neutering can be the answer to these behaviors in both sexes, and we will look at this in more detail in the chapter 'Adolescence'.

One or two?

If you are considering more than one Yorkie, it would be best to get one at a time. That way you could get a feel for the breed, and the time, cost and effort required, before taking on another one. Without the distraction of a sibling, your puppy is also likely to form a stronger bond with you as its leader.

Companion dog or something more?

Do you have expectations of your Yorkie as a show dog or for breeding? If you do, you will need to do in-depth research into the parents' natures, their abilities and their breeding.

TIMING

The best time to pick up your puppy

As well as getting an idea of the sort of puppy you're looking for, you need to decide on the best time to bring a puppy home. This should be at the beginning of a stretch when you, or most of the family, will be around and able to care for it full-time for most of the day. If you're retired this mightn't be a consideration, but if you're a working family with school-going children, for example, you should try to pick your puppy up early in the school holidays.

The weather is another consideration. If you live in a country where the summer and winter temperatures are very different, or the wet seasons are extreme, then getting your puppy at the start of a warm or dry season will make for much easier toilet training.

Luckily, any breeders in your area are likely to have taken these factors into consideration, so you will find that the most puppies are available at the start of summer and the long school holidays.

No puppy of **any** breed should leave its mother before eight weeks of age, but because Yorkies are still very small then, good breeders won't let their puppies go to their new homes before they are at least 12 weeks, and some will insist on keeping them until 16. Respect this waiting time, because this is when the puppies are building their immune systems and learning important life lessons from their mothers and litter mates.

Once you've decided when it will be most convenient to bring a new puppy home, work back these 12-16 weeks to figure out ideally when your prospective puppy will be, or will have been, born. Ideally you want to visit the litter at around the eight-week mark.

When to start looking

Many breeders advertise litters as soon as the mother is pregnant, so it's wise not to leave your search to the last few weeks. If you're looking for a family pet, your search shouldn't take more than a few months. However, if you're looking for a dog that is competition- or breeding-quality you could be looking for up to two years before actually bringing your puppy home. You might be in contact with a breeder before the litter is born, or even before the mother is mated.

But no matter when you start your search, it should begin with identifying the most responsible route to finding puppies for sale in your area.

THE BREEDER

Those first crucial weeks

Your puppy will spend the crucial first three months of her life with the breeder, which means the breeder plays a huge role in shaping her temperament, character and behavior. Choosing the right breeder and buying responsibly is one of the most important decisions you will make in choosing your puppy.

BUYING RESPONSIBLY

There is an alarming amount of puppy farming going on out there (as well as right here under our noses). Puppy farmers are high-volume breeders who breed puppies with little or no consideration for the health and wellbeing of the puppies or their parents. Motivated by profit, they ignore guidelines on the safe maximum number of litters per dog, and typically separate puppies from their mothers too early. The mothers and puppies live in conditions ranging from substandard to awful, then the puppies are moved to normal-looking homes for viewings – homes which are, in reality, nothing more than shop fronts.

So when arranging to see a litter, please make sure it's with a responsible breeder. You want to be certain you are buying a healthy, happy puppy and, at the same time, not unknowingly supporting the cruel puppy trade.

And stay away from breeders advertising 'tea cup' or 'tiny toy' Yorkies. These terms vaguely indicate a predicted weight range; and in any case very small Yorkies, weighing under 4 lbs (1.8kg) as adults, are far more prone to health issues and genetic disorders.

Local and online adverts might seem like the obvious place to start your puppy search, but good breeders will be accredited with at least one reputable organization. Better to start with these:

- the websites of the Kennel Club in your country
  Breeders approved by the AKC or the Kennel Club (UK), for example, agree to certain welfare standards, to produce puppies in line with the breed standards, and also to reduce or eradicate genetic illnesses.
- Yorkshire Terrier clubs
- trainers and breeders at dog shows
- dog trainers and behavior experts
- vets.

Make a list of breeders based close enough to your home for you to be able to visit the litter at least once and pick up your puppy in person.

First contact

Now to make the call. (Emailing is your next best option, but you will learn so much more by speaking to the breeder in person.) These are some key questions to ask:

- Did you breed the puppies yourself?
    It's imperative they did so you can meet the mother.
- How many puppies are, or were there, in the litter?
    This is to avoid seeing just one puppy. You want to make sure you see all the puppies together so you can compare them and see how they interact.
- If I visit, will I see all the puppies together with their mother, in the place where they were bred?
    This should be a 'yes' and that is where you need to meet the mother as well as the litter.
- For how long have you owned and bred Yorkshire Terriers?

- Is it only Yorkies that you breed?

  Ideally, this should be 'yes'. Multi-breed breeders are more likely to be backyard breeders or puppy farmers.

- Are you registered with the Kennel Club or a member of any breed clubs?

  If they are, be sure to check their answers for yourself after the call.

- How old is the mother? And is this her first litter?

  She should be over 18 months old, and no more than seven years. She should have had no more than four litters in her lifetime, and no more than one litter in the space of a year.

- What will happen to the mother when you've finished breeding with her?

  Ideally she will stay part of her already-loving home.

- How do the parent dogs compare to the Yorkshire Terrier breed standard?

  If they don't know about the standard, or make light of it, you should stay away.

- Have the puppies or their mother had any health problems?

- What health screening has been done for both parents?

  You want to know if there are any hereditary health problems that could affect the puppies going forward. There is more on this in the next chapter, 'The paperwork'. If the breeder doesn't believe in health testing, stay away.

- At what age do you recommend your puppies leave you for their new homes?

  This should not be before 12 weeks.

- How many people interact with the puppies on a daily basis?

  Ideally you want the puppies to be experiencing the comings and goings of a family household.

- Will they have been treated for worms before they leave for their new homes?

  They should have received at least one deworming treatment by then.

- Will they have been given their first vaccinations?

  Vaccination requirements vary from country to country, but initial vaccinations generally comprise two doses with an interval of two to four weeks. The first of these is usually given around eight weeks.

- Will they have they been microchipped?

  This is a tiny chip injected under your puppy's skin at the back of her neck. It holds her unique number which links to your contact details and, unlike a collar and tag, it stays there for life. In the UK it is law for all puppies to have been microchipped by eight weeks old.

- Do you have the relevant paperwork?

  The breeder must be able to give you a record of any vaccinations as this will need to be seen by the vet, as well as taken to any training classes or boarding kennels. They must also give you the details of microchipping, if relevant, so you can change the contact details to your own. If there are any registration and pedigree certificates, you should be able to see these too, along with any health screening results.

There are a lot of questions to ask, and you don't want this to come across like an interrogation. But you

are taking on a new family member who could be with you for the next 12-plus years. You will be spending a lot of money, and probably traveling a long distance. These questions needn't all be answered in the first call, but they **are** legitimate and a good breeder will be understanding, or appreciative even.

A good and responsible breeder:

- will be happy to answer all your questions on the phone.
- will ask questions of you too, to make sure their puppies are going to excellent homes.
- will have photos and possibly video clips of the puppies' parents, and be happy to send you more by phone or email if you feel you need them (especially if a visit means a lengthy journey on your part).
- will give you the impression of actively loving and nurturing each pup, as well as the mother, to make sure they are well socialized.
- will be happy to arrange a time for you to visit the puppies and their mother in the place where they were born and raised.
- will be happy for you to have more than one visit before pick-up if you feel you need it.
- might give you references of people who've bought puppies from them in the past.
- might give you some form of guarantee against genetic illnesses.
- might offer to take the dog back if you can't keep it. Some breeders even include a contract requiring you to contact them first if you should ever need to give it up.

A responsible breeder will NEVER:

- offer to deliver the puppy to you.
- offer to meet you at a random place.
- tell you the mother is out at the vets, or for any other reason. If she isn't there, the puppy most likely wasn't bred there, or there could be a problem with the mother.
- set up the visit so you will see just one puppy. (You should always see the puppies together.)
- tell you the litter has been vaccinated before four weeks of age.
- advise you to take a puppy before 12 (or at least ten) weeks of age.
- suggest that you breed your puppy for money.
- push you for payment.

Adverts

If you have had no luck finding a litter through breed clubs and dog experts, then have a look at online adverts, but these are some early puppy-farmer warning signs.

- They often use the same contact number on more than one advert. If the advert is posted on the internet, do a search on the number to see if it has been used on any other puppy adverts.
- They often use the same descriptions, word-for-word, in more than one advert. Search a key phrase in the wording to locate duplicate advertising.
- Photos of the puppies or the parents may also have been used in other adverts.

Price

Don't look for a bargain – good and responsibly bred Yorkies aren't cheap. But be just as wary of puppies priced over the average, because silly money can never guarantee you a miracle dog. Don't be fooled by promises of 'free puppy packs' either – they don't necessarily make the seller any more legitimate.

NEVER get a puppy if you have any doubts about the seller or breeder.

Once you've found a breeder you are sure is responsible and caring, and you've identified a litter of puppies you like the look and sound of, and you're as sure as you can be that they're healthy, happy and from a good home environment, set up your visit or visits.

Then find or buy a small, soft blanket to take with you. This is so that, if you **do** reserve a puppy, you can leave it with her until you pick her up. It will absorb the smells of mom and the litter mates until then, and help to make the separation less stressful.

TIP
Let this soft, comfy blanket absorb the smells of you, your house and your family before you go. Put it in with the dirty laundry for a few hours. That should do the trick!

Then the countdown begins …

... well almost.

4. THE PAPERWORK

First there's the inevitable paperwork to consider.

All paperwork can be subject to faking; nothing can guarantee how your dog will turn out; and anyway there's no reason your Yorkie shouldn't be a wonderful companion without any paperwork at all. But checking the paperwork is an excellent way to minimize the risk.

If it can be sent electronically, aim to see as much of it as you can before the first visit. In summary, this is what the breeder should have shown or given you before you take your puppy home.

Health certifications and ratings

Even if you don't plan on breeding or competing in showing classes, it's important to check the health clearance certificates and ratings for both parents.

- **Essential tests:**
  - Ophthalmologist evaluations (eye tests, dated within the past year)
  - Patella evaluations (for luxating patella, which is a dislocation of the kneecaps)

- **Recommended tests:**
  Although these are not essential, the breeder might also have arranged testing for:
  - Legg-Calve-Perthes (a disorder of the hip joint),
  - Autoimmune thyroiditis (a thyroid malfunction)
  - Liver shunt (a liver problem common in Yorkies).

Health guarantees

Some breeders will supply a guarantee with their pups that covers them against certain health problems.

Vaccination and deworming records

You will need this paperwork to take to your own vet, as well as to any training classes your puppy might attend or kennels she might need to board at.

Microchipping details

If the puppies have been microchipped, you will need your puppy's individual number and the name of the provider so you can change the existing contact details to your own.

Registration papers (where applicable)

These are the certificates that record your puppy's registration number and serve as proof of her ancestry. If applicable, you should be able to see these either by email or on your first visit. Ideally they will have been issued by a reputable registry like your national Kennel Club, but beware of smaller, lesser-known registries which sometimes register dogs without proof of pure breeding.

Pedigree documents (where applicable)

These show your dog's family tree and list the breeding decisions that have been made. Pedigree papers are less official than the registration papers because a dog that is registered is always a pedigree, but a pedigree dog is not necessarily registered.

Sales contract

You might want to see the sales contract that will need to be signed by both parties on pick-up.

5. TIME TO CHOOSE

When the day arrives you'll be eager to get going, but before you set off, remember to take that soft blanket to leave with the puppies in case you do decide to take one of them.

WHICH PUPPY?

You'll be itching to spend time with the puppies, I know, but try not to let down your instantly-falling-in-love guard. Not just yet.

Basic checks

First try to make sense of the puppies' environment. Is it warm, friendly and homely? You want to be as sure as you can that this is where they've grown up. Watch how the breeder interacts with the puppies too. Ideally there should be indications that they are being bought up right underfoot and getting lots of human contact. And if you were promised any paperwork, ask to see it.

The mother

Spend some time with her. She must be friendly and good-natured if that is what you hope for in your puppy. You should also consider whether she is the actual mother because sadly this does need checking. Does she look like she's just had the litter? And does she interact with the puppies?

The puppies

FINALLY. You can immerse yourself in the writhing bundle of fluffy heart-melters. But keep your wits about you. Study their temperaments and make sure they are:

- happy and confident,
- friendly and interactive,
- and interested in you and everything around them.

And make sure they look healthy.

- Their noses should be clean, cool and damp, and their breathing should be quiet.
- Their eyes should be clear and bright, with no sign of discharge.
- The ears should be clean and not smelly.
- There should be no irritation around the genitals or bottom, or signs of diarrhea.
- The coat should be clean, with no bald patches or greasiness.
- They should walk and run with no difficulty.

Which puppy?

All still going well, you can start choosing. But which one? There are no right or wrong puppies, just ones that are more or less suited to you, your family and your other pets. For example, if you already have a dominant dog, a submissive puppy would be a sensible choice. Here are some tips that could help you with your decision:

- Don't rush this. Sit down with the puppies and spend all the time you need with them.
- If you are absolutely sure you want a boy, you could ask the breeder to remove the girls while you meet the boys, or vice versa.
- Play with each one to see how they interact with

you. If you play with one then turn away, does it follow you? If not, it is likely to be more independent than a puppy that does.

- Distance yourself and study their energy levels. Some will be more active than others and need more exercise. If you want to walk out lots and play games, choose the busy puppy, and if you lead a quiet life and want cuddles, choose one with a laid-back personality.
- Watch how they interact with their litter mates. This could be an indication of how easy they will be to socialize. For example, if another puppy yelps, do they stop playing quite so roughly? If they play nicely they are more likely to grow into adult dogs that play well with other dogs.
- Sort out which are more dominant and which more submissive. The more dominant puppies will take food and toys from the others, and only seem really happy when they are on top of the pile while play fighting. More submissive puppies will play happily with their litter mates without trying to dominate. They will allow other dogs to win a toy, or back off when other puppies want the food or a toy.
- Tell the breeder about your family and any other pets, and ask them for their opinion, because they should have experience with the breed and will also have had time to get to know the individual puppies.
- Make a noise behind the puppies. Clap your hands for example. If they flinch, that might be a sign of a nervous disposition, and if they don't react, it could be an indication of poor hearing.

- Throw something to see if they run after it, or bring it back.
- As a test, try placing the puppies on their backs and gently resting your fingers on their chests. The puppies that struggle to get free are less patient than the ones that make little effort to get away.

A good choice is an even-tempered puppy with an outgoing nature. But it's often said that you don't choose your dog or puppy, it chooses you, and many people vouch for this. One puppy might spend your entire visit convincing you she's the one you want to take home, and if that's the case, she probably is.

Whichever pup you choose, when you've settled on your choice, that will be the best dog in the world, and time after time you will ask yourself how you got to be **so** lucky.

Before you leave

(assuming you're coming back for the puppy at a later date)

- **Identity** – Make sure you and the breeder can tell which one is yours. For example, the owner might put a colored collar on your puppy.
- **Deposit** – The breeder will most likely ask for a deposit to secure your puppy. Make sure that you get a receipt and a written agreement that the contract is only binding if the puppy is in good health when you collect it.
- **Sales contract** – Confirm with the breeder that they will have a puppy contract ready at the time of collection. This should include details of health screening (for the puppy and its parents); details of the parents; all information to date on vaccinations,

deworming, micro-chipping and veterinary visits; and a health guarantee (if applicable).

- **Food and care** – Find out whatever you can about meals. What are the puppies being fed at the moment? How much and how often? Ask to see the food so you can be sure of giving her exactly what she is used to when you bring her home.

Finally, ask the breeder if you can leave your soft puppy blanket with the litter so that when you pick her up, you will be able to bring all those familiar mommy-puppy smells with her into her new home.

6. PREPARING FOR THE BIG DAY

It almost goes without saying that when you pick up your bundle of joy, and trouble, you will need buckets of love, oodles of patience and a fantastic sense of humor. But you will also need to do a surprising amount of planning, puppy-proofing and purchasing of paraphernalia.

Things to do

- Arrange a date to pick up your puppy when it has passed the 12-week mark. If you will be traveling by car, it should be a day when at least one other person can accompany the driver.
- Book a visit to the vet for about two days after pick-up.
- If you will be taking out pet insurance, do your homework now so you can have it in place as soon as you bring your puppy home.
- Puppy proof your home, checking every nook and cranny:
  - Secure the property. This is the most important thing you can do to keep your puppy safe. If you have a yard or garden, ensure the wall or fence is escape proof from the ground up. If you have an apartment with a balcony, make sure there is no way she could get through any railings, or up and over a low wall.

- If there is a pool, pond or any deep water she could fall into, fence it off.
- Check that there are no chemicals within reach (pesticides, weedkillers, fertilizers, etc).
- Cover or hide electricity cables and wires.
- Tie up or pack away anything that could topple over or be pulled by a cord or cable.
- Remove sharp objects and small things she could choke on.
- Be aware of any plants in your house and yard or garden that may be poisonous. It's worth checking online for a comprehensive list, but these are some of the more common varieties: Aloe Vera, Asparagus Fern, Azalea, Castor Bean, Corn Cockle, Crocus, Cyclamen, Daffodil, Holly Berry, Foxglove, Ivy (Hedera Helix), Jade (Crassula Ovata), Jerusalem Cherry, Jessamine, Hyacinth, Lily of the Valley, Milkweed, Mistletoe, Oleander, Philodendron, Rhododendron, Tulip, Water Hemlock.
- Remove valuables from the floor.

- Decide on her special place, a suitable comfy space that she can make her own. This is where her crate will be positioned if you choose to use one, or her play pen, or simply her basket and toys. This special place should be somewhere central – somewhere that she can feel safe, but without feeling isolated or excluded. An ideal position would be against a wall in the room that most of you spend the most time in during the day. If you already have another dog, it should be away from your other dog's special place, at least for starters.

Things to buy, make or borrow

- **Small soft blanket** – if you left this with the litter when you chose your puppy, be sure to collect it when you pick her up. Those familiar smells will help makes the transition far less stressful.
- **Crate (also commonly referred to as a cage or den)** – this is optional of course, but it would serve as your puppy's own space, a special place where she can be safe, quiet and keep her toys. There is more about this in the next three chapters, but for now choose one that is just big enough for your puppy's basket or bed, a couple of toys and her bowls. Wire cages are better ventilated than plastic ones, offer better views, and are easily collapsible.
- **Comfortable dog bed** – this could be a basket, a dog cushion or even a folded blanket, as long as it is soft, comfortable and easily washable.
- **Harness** – when walking your Yorkie, the lead should be clipped onto a harness rather than a collar to avoid unnecessary pressure on her neck. There are essentially two types of harness for Toy breeds: the strap harness which clips on and is adjustable, and the vest or wrap harness which is worn like a vest and has a clip on the upper back for the lead. Whichever type you choose, make sure it is soft and comfortable, lightweight and durable.
- **Collar** – even with a harness, and even if she is microchipped, you might still want your Yorkie to wear a collar to hold her ID tag in case she gets loose or lost. Choose one that is soft, lightweight and comfortable.
- **ID tag** – keep it small and light and have it engraved with her name and your contact details.

- **Short lead (four to six feet long)** – again, nice and light.
- **Extendable lead** – these can make walks more enjoyable for you and your puppy. However, they can be dangerous, so should be used carefully and only once your puppy is walking nicely on the short lead.
- **Bowls** – go for a small-breed, non-tip, non-slip design, ideally in stainless steel or ceramic. You might also consider a non-spill travel bowl for car trips, and a crate bowl that clips onto the door or side of your puppy's crate so that it can't be overturned.
- **Food** – start with the diet your puppy has been on at her breeders. After that you can move her on to the food of your choice. If you are concerned about making the best decision, consult your vet at her first check-up.
- **Treats** – you will need lots of these. They are fantastic motivators when your puppy is first learning the rules, and excellent for reinforcing good behavior. Choose treats that are suitable for small-breed puppies and avoid additives and preservatives, including sugar and salt. As a rule of thumb, the fewer ingredients the better.
- **Treat pouch** – a handy pocket for loose treats that keeps your own pockets from constantly smelling of dog food. Another option is a tiny sealable tub that you can shake the treats in noisily to get her attention.
- **Chews** – your puppy will spend around four hours of each day munching on things, so it's up to you to provide what you want her to do her chewing on.

Chews make a fabulous alternative to table legs and leather shoes, but with a young puppy avoid any chews that can splinter. Antler horns are good, and so are Kong toys filled with treats.

- **Toys** – Can a puppy have too many toys? I think not. Invest in plenty of toys in all shapes, sizes, textures, colors and smells. She will chew on them, play with them and even snuggle up with them for hours. (It's wise to avoid giving her old shoes because, smart as she is, she's unlikely to differentiate between old and new when she slips inside your shoe closet.)
- **Anti-chew or citronella** – it's worth investing in either of these to spray onto those things she absolutely must not chew on. Expensive chair legs for example.
- **Poo(p) bags** – choose biodegradable ones.
- **Newspaper** – or equivalent wee-mat material for house-training
- **Carpet cleaner and odor eliminator** – buy these separately or as one product, but make sure it's 'pet friendly'.
- **Hot water bottle** – strong and well covered
- **Grooming kit** – a soft brush and comb, dog nail clippers, and a quality dog shampoo. There's an abundance of hair- and body-care products available for Yorkies, ranging from paw wax to skin sprays, and lotions to electric clippers. Some are useful and others are pure indulgence, but there's no need for any of these at this stage.
- **Dental care kit** – a dog finger toothbrush for 'Toy breeds', a three-sided toothbrush and dog toothpaste.

- **Dog gates/baby gates/stair gates** – these are far better than closed doors for keeping a room off-limits. There's a huge choice on the market, but make sure the bars are close enough together for your small-breed puppy, and stay away from stretch gates that she could get stuck in.
- **Exercise pen/play pen** – this is useful if you are leaving her for a couple of hours because it is big enough (usually about four feet by four feet) for her to sleep, play and poop in if necessary.
- **Pet carrier bag/sling/backpack** – in case you're planning to take her out and about with you.
- **Car seat, pet travel carrier or dog guard** – if she is likely to travel by car you will need a safe form of restraint. Raised booster seats are a good choice for Toy dogs, and also good for dogs that suffer from motion sickness.

Setting the rules

Before you bring your newest family member home, it's essential for you and the other members of the household to have a serious chat about the rules. Decide among yourselves where your puppy will be allowed, and when. Make sure you are all in agreement about which rooms and pieces of furniture are off-limit. And make sure everyone understands that sneaking the puppy into an off-limit area, or letting it break the rules in any other way, would only be unfair on the puppy in the long run.

Choosing a name

You could choose this once your puppy is home, but either way her name is more important than you might think. You will be using it several times a day for years to come so it must be something she will easily recognize.

- Dogs respond better to shorter names – one-syllable names with a hard consonant or consonants like Pip or Zac for example, or two-syllable names such as Bu-ddy or Cor-ky. You might love the name Jemima or Octavia, but your dog would thank you for calling her Jem or Otto instead.
- Make sure the name you choose doesn't sound too much like a commonly-used command: No, Sit, Down, Stay, Come, Here, Good or Fetch. Beau and Jo, for example, sound too much like No.
- And don't choose a name that sounds like that of another member of the household. If your mother is called Anne, don't call the puppy Dan; if your cat is Tigger, don't call it Digger or Trigger.
- Choose a name that is easy to call out. 'M' and 'n' sounds are soft which makes them more difficult to call out loud than harder consonants like 'b', 't' and 'z'. Molly, say, is a less effective pet name than Pippy.
- Never give any dog a name you wouldn't be happy calling out loud in public.

7. PICKING UP YOUR PUPPY

'Happiness is a warm puppy'
Charles M Schulz

The big day has finally arrived. If possible, pick her up early in the day so she can spend lots of time in her new environment before facing her first night without her mother and litter mates.

If you are driving, try to take someone with you to comfort her, but don't take too many people because the journey should be calm and quiet.

Before you go

- If you haven't already set up her special place in a safe but central spot, do that now. Crate or no crate, furnish it with the comfortable dog basket or bed, some toys, and also some treats if you like.

- And if you haven't already sprayed your most valued furniture with anti-chew, now's a very good time.

Things to take

- The remainder of the payment (if necessary)
- An absorbent mat (or similar protection) in case she relieves herself in the car
- Poo bags and cleaning cloths
- Two bowls (one for food and one for water)
- A small amount of food (in a container)
- A bottle of water
- A small selection of toys and chews
- A backup soft blanket or cushion is also a good idea (in case something has happened to the one you left with the breeder)
- A harness and your lead (not extendable)
- A travel crate (if that's your preference) with an item of clothing inside that smells of you.

The big moment

There at last and this is it! Give your new family member and best friend a gently gargantuan cuddle, then have a play and check that she's still in good health:

- happy, confident and curious,
- that there are no signs of mucus from the nose, bottom or genitals,
- and that her ears are clean and not smelly.

In the excitement

Apart from your new and perfect puppy, don't forget to come away with:

- the blanket you left, if you left one
- the relevant paperwork including:
  - a receipt of payment
  - health records detailing check-ups and procedures, including the vaccination certificate
  - microchip details if relevant (so you can register the puppy under your name).

It's also worth double checking her food type (just in case it's changed) and finding out what times she has been having her meals.

And last but definitely not least, remember to thank the mother as well as the breeder for your beautiful puppy.

Traveling

Make sure your puppy is feeling safe and happy to be with you before you take her away for good. She is totally reliant on you now, so put yourself into those tiny little paws that are being taken away from their mother and litter mates. Realize that she is leaving the only place she has ever known and, if you're driving, getting into a car for the first time too! Ask yourself, "How would I be feeling now?" and "What would I need from this new person or family?" You'd want to feel safe and secure, loved and cherished.

Put her harness on before you set off. This is best done with two people so one of you can hold and distract her while the other puts it on. You don't want it too tight or too loose. You should just be able to put two fingers between your puppy and the harness at any point.

If you're traveling by car, the puppy would be happiest being held by the passenger in the back seat. She would need to be held securely (legally speaking 'suitably restrained'), so that the driver is not distracted, and be given love and constant reassurance on the journey. However, where you put her in the car will depend on the laws in your country or state, as holding her in the back seat could affect your insurance.

If you've brought a travel crate instead, then arrange the comfy blanket inside, with its scents of mom and the litter mates, as well as the item of clothing you've been wearing so she can get used to your scent too. Place her gently inside and fasten the seatbelt over the crate. The passenger should sit next to the crate to comfort her. She will probably be too anxious for toys, but she should be offered them anyway.

If the journey home is a long one, you'll need to stop every hour, or more if you can. Like people, dogs can suffer from travel sickness, so it is possible she might be feeling a little ill or even be sick on the journey. She will also need these breaks for a walk and the chance to go to the toilet, but always keep her on the lead. Though she's unlikely to stray from you, this would be a terrible place for her to get loose.

At every break, offer her some of the food and water in the bowls you've brought along.

8. THE HOMECOMING

Before going into the house or apartment, give her a chance to wee.

And if you have another dog or other dogs she hasn't yet met, you should stay outside while you introduce them. There is a section in the next chapter on how to do this safely and sensibly.

When you're ready, carry her into the house and put her in the special place you've created for her, or in her crate with the door wide open. Sit beside her, arrange the blanket smelling of her mother and litter mates in her basket, and give her a treat.

When she's explored her special place, let her venture into all the areas of the house she will be allowed in, so that she knows this is home. She will be feeling overwhelmed, nervous even, so stay close by her side, a reassuring presence. If there are areas of the house that will be off limits to her, then it is better not to let her in there from the start than to change the rules at some later stage.

All the treats today should be given in her crate or special area – her very own bedroom. Her comfy blanket should stay there and it is advisable to feed her there too. Do everything you can think of to make her feel that this is the best and safest place in the world. If there is a crate and the design is very open, cover it with a blanket leaving gaps she can see out of.

Puppies need to wee about once an hour and poop several times a day, so take her outside, or to her potty space, every hour if you can. She will still piddle and poop wherever and whenever she needs to because she is so little, can't talk to you, and has no idea that in some places this is a no-no. Toilet training is covered in more detail later on, but for now be sure to clean up after her very well, always using an odor eliminator.

At this stage, she will be needing up to 18 hours' sleep a day, and today she is likely to need even more than usual, so try not to overload her senses with too many people or too much excitement. But your presence is essential for her peace of mind so, when you're sitting quietly, let her sit with you and sleep on your lap or close by. If she is shivering, keep her warm.

Make sure there is always fresh water available to her, and that she knows where it is. Feed her what she is used to and, as far as practical, at the times she is used to. She might not want to eat at first and that's okay, she'll eat when she's ready. Take the food away and re-present it to her a little later.

Aim to give her her last meal of the day a good two hours before her bedtime, so she has a chance to go to the toilet before settling down for the first night.

9. NEW PUPPY SAFETY

The best way to keep your puppy safe is through your and your family's and housemates' own diligence.

- Handle her gently and carry her carefully.
- Be mindful of doors. Keep them closed and open where necessary, and don't shut them too quickly – your new 'shadow' could be right on your heels.
- Make a habit of looking where you're walking too. She might've been sleeping in the next room just two seconds ago, but that's no reason to assume she's still there now.
- Teach yourself to check under cushions, throws and blankets before you sit down.
- Don't let her near high balconies, low window ledges, unsecured staircases, cars or lawnmowers.
- Keep her away from unfenced water.
- Cover or hide electricity cables, wires and cords. Apart from shock there is the danger of pulling something down on top of her (a heavy iron or a boiling kettle).
- Be careful with rocking or reclining chairs.
- Minimize her jumping on and off high furniture to protect her joints in the long term.
- Supervise her carefully when she's playing with children and other dogs.

Small children

If you have small children, it's important to supervise them when they're with your puppy. They must understand NOW that she is NOT a toy.

- They must not be allowed to pick her up without adult supervision.
- They must not be allowed to disturb her if she is sleeping or has taken herself to a quiet place.
- They must not run around squealing, and if the puppy becomes over-excited they must keep still.
- They should be allowed to play calm games, but nothing involving wrestling or tugging.

OTHER PETS

Your other dog (if you have one)

- Keep introductions short and sweet to start with, with both dogs on a lead.
- If possible, let them meet for the first time away from home. Ideally, choose somewhere your older

dog hasn't been before so that the excitement of the new environment will dilute the puppy's presence. If your puppy is not yet protected by her vaccinations, try to ensure the meeting place is somewhere no other dogs are likely to go.

- Stand still or walk slowly when you let your puppy and your older dog meet, and try not to interfere.
- When you get home, if you have a yard or garden, let the dogs meet there again in the same way before going inside. Then let your puppy into the house first, before letting the older dog in.
- Lift any pre-existing dog toys and food bowls off the floor for a few days.
- If you are worried about your puppy's safety, use a baby gate or stair gate to separate the dogs in the short term, or put the puppy in her crate or a playpen while the dogs get used to each other.
- Make sure all members of the family give the older dog more attention than usual.
- Feed your puppy in her special place for now. Even later, when your dogs are fed together, their eating places should be at least six feet apart.

Multiple dogs

If you already have more than one other dog, the process is the same but it's imperative that you introduce the puppy to just one dog at a time.

Cats

When your puppy is this young, she is unlikely to be a problem for your cat. But, to be on the safe side, introduce them with care.

- Keep your puppy on a lead when they first meet, and have a lovely treat ready. If your cat responds by hissing to begin with, your puppy will most likely retreat. But if the cat runs away, be ready to distract the puppy with the treat so she doesn't chase after it.

- If the introduction becomes unpleasant, separate them and try again later. They could be at odds for several weeks until they reach an agreement.
- Always restrain your puppy around the cat until she learns that the cat is not something to be chased.
- Distract her with a toy to teach her that playing with people is more fun than chasing the cat. It's debatable, but that's what we want her to think.
- If you need to keep your puppy and the cat apart while you're out, use the crate, pen or a stair gate.
- Make sure the cat has safe places high up that it can reach instead of having to run away.

CURIOUS THINGS

Your puppy will be chewing on everything now, using her mouth to find out about the world around her. But there are some 'curiosities' it's particularly important to keep out of her reach:

Non-edibles

- Medication – human medication is the biggest cause of pet poisoning
- Human vitamin supplements
- Anti-freeze and other chemicals – many of these are sweet-tasting
- Paint thinner
- Pesticides, weedkillers and fertilizers
- Toothpaste

- Sponges
- Household cleaners (including toilet cleaners)
- A surprisingly high number of household and garden plants can be poisonous when eaten in large amounts. (See the shortlist and advice in 'Preparing for the big day'.)
- Small metal objects like coins, and nuts and bolts
- Pins, needles and other sharp objects.

People food

It's always best to feed your puppy or dog actual puppy or dog food, and simply stay clear of treats from your own plate. But there are some people foods that you must never let her get hold of, never mind feed her, because while they are perfectly safe for human consumption, they are poisonous and potentially fatal to dogs. These include:

- Chocolate (especially dark chocolate)
- Anything containing Xylitol (artificial sweetener, commonly used in sweets and gum, but also in some sweet foods like low-calorie cake)
- Alcohol
- Onion
- Garlic
- Grapes or raisins
- Avocado.

Also keep her away from

- Soft or cooked bones (especially chicken or pork), as they could get stuck in her throat)
- Sausage and other processed meats that contain preservatives
- Macadamia nuts

- Fruit pips or seeds
- Potato peels or green potatoes
- Rhubarb leaves
- Baker's yeast or yeast dough
- Caffeine
- Mushrooms
- Hops (generally in beer).

Dog products

Don't assume everything at a pet shop will be puppy-friendly. Avoid:
- Cow hooves, which can splinter, and raw hide and pigs' ears which can be a choking hazard
- Toweling fabrics that become stringy when chewed
- Toys that might become stringy when chewed
- Chew toys made of plastic or soft rubber
- Toys with small parts they could choke on.

Call the vet immediately if you suspect your puppy has eaten something potentially harmful.

Put yourself in your puppy's paws

If you want to be really proactive, put yourself in her itchy little paws and busy jaws for a moment. Being careful not to underestimate her size, determination or intelligence, get down on all fours and examine every nook and cranny to see what temptations call. Then take these away. Get everything out of her reach. Make it as difficult as you can for her to get into any form of danger or trouble.

Then watch over her, just as you would a busy toddler.

10. THE FIRST NIGHT

Crunch time! She's had her supper, a couple of hours ago, and it's time for bed.

Take her outside for a last chance to go to the toilet. Stay with her in the place you'd most like her to go, and, be patient.

Using a crate or special place

Back inside, make sure her crate or safe space is as appealing as possible, with her comfortable bed and her soft blanket. (In the short term, some people make this space in their bedrooms, setting it up by the side of their beds. Considering the trauma of this first night, to your puppy and yourselves, there is a lot to be said for this. She still wouldn't be able to snuggle up the way she's used to, but at least she could see you and hear you and would know she's not alone.)

If her sleeping place is a metal crate, the openness still leaves your puppy quite exposed, so if you haven't already done so, put a blanket over all or part of it, making sure she can always see out.

It's a good idea to make a warm, but not too warm, hot water bottle, and wrap it carefully into her comfy blanket. This is to replicate the body warmth of her mother and litter mates when they're snuggled up. You could also put a ticking clock in the bed to mimic a heartbeat. And if the special place is not in your room, consider leaving a radio playing softly to give her the sense she is not alone.

Scatter some toys and treats and make sure she has access to clean water in her non-tip or clip-on bowl.

If the space is big enough to include a place to relieve herself, aside from the bedding and bowls, then cover this with newspaper or an absorbent wee mat.

When crunch time comes, don't fuss over her. Just put her in her crate or special place with a treat, as though she's the luckiest puppy in the world, and close the door: be it a cage door, room door or baby gate.

In all likelihood she will cry at first, but resist the urge to pick her up. If that's where you want her at night, she must learn to stay in her crate or special place from day one. In fact, it's far kinder not to give her any attention when she cries, because any time you 'give in' would just encourage her to cry even harder each time you had to step away again. You're the one who needs to be strong, for her sake. Know that she is warm, comfortable, fed and tired, and the cries should soon subside. What's more, if you persevere, she will soon come to like the safety and quiet of her own space.

Sleeping in your bed or the crate? Debate

It's not unlikely that your puppy will soon decide that your bed is the most comfortable place in the world, and that cuddling up next to you, on or even in your bed, is the best and safest way to spend the nights. Yes, she's not stupid and, what's more, many Yorkie owners are fine with this. Many argue that letting her cry is heartless and unnatural, and it certainly does feel that way at the time.

It's up to you of course, but here are some reasons why her crate or special area is a good idea, at least to start off with.

- She's not yet toilet trained, and accidents in your bed are a great deal more difficult to clean up than accidents in her special place.
- There is the risk of her falling off the bed and getting a fright or even an injury.
- When she is this tiny, there is, albeit small, the danger of your rolling onto her during the night.
- If you're a couple, her sleeping on the bed could get in the way of your own together time.
- Once she's started sleeping on the bed, this would be a very difficult habit to break.

What about toilet time?

If she is in your bedroom, whether in a crate or on your bed, and you hear her shuffling around in the night, get up straight away and take her outside, or to the place you'd most like her to go. She's likely to avoid messing in her sleeping place if she can help it.

If she's not in your room, you'll need to set an alarm for the middle of the night so you can get up and take her out. Alternatively, and only if you've laid down a wee mat, you could wait until very early the next morning.

At some stage she won't need this break at all, but whichever option you choose, you'll need to keep this up for the next few weeks at least.

11. THE FIRST WEEK

From just three weeks old your puppy has been socializing and learning to play with her mother and litter mates. Now suddenly she must learn to be with you, and with people, and to figure out a whole new set of rules. Luckily for you she is at her most impressionable during these early days, so the time and effort you put in now to building a positive relationship will be worth buckets of good behavior over the months and years to come.

For her own sense of security, as well as your relationship going forward, she needs to learn straight away that you are the leader, and quickly come to understand her position in the household. Mesmerizingly cute as she is, you need to be firm with her from the start, and consistent in your demands; **never** harsh or aggressive.

We will look at discipline and obedience later on but until you've read that far, if she does something you don't want her to do, don't punish her or show aggression in any form. That would only confuse her and make her fearful.

Instead:

1. distract her
2. encourage her to do something else, something good
3. then reward her for listening.

Encourage and reward – praise her at every opportunity for the good things she does in your eyes, so she can begin to learn what is right in your world.

Be clear and consistent in your praise and she will become the most doting and loyal friend you could ever imagine.

Love her

Unconditionally. Do this and the rest will come naturally.

Teach her her name

Use her name to get her attention, and reward her when she responds to it. But be careful not to say it over and over again or she will quickly become de-sensitized to it.

Keep her special place appealing

Even if she is sleeping on your bed at night, she will still need this crate or special place during the day – to keep her out of trouble if you nip out, or to keep her safe from your existing pets or small children.

All associations with her special place should be positive, so it should never be used for punishment. Make it comfortable and leave toys and treats inside so that it always feels welcoming and homely. If she soils in it, clean it well.

Encourage her into her special place and praise her when she goes in on her own.

Feed and water her

Your puppy should be having three (or maybe four) meals a day at this stage, ideally of the same food she was having with the other puppies in the litter. If you don't know how much to feed her, work out her daily allowance from the instructions on the food packaging. Split this allowance into three or four equal portions and work out a schedule for regular feeding, for example:

- Three feeds: 7am, 12.30pm and 6pm
- Four feeds: 7am, 11am, 3pm and 7pm.

If she's on dry puppy food, you can add a little warm water and let it soak for a few minutes before feeding her. This makes it easier to eat and digest.

If you have more than one dog, feed them separately – at least six feet apart – to prevent food aggression.

You, or her primary carer if it's not you, should feed her most often. Feed her some of her meal by hand as this encourages trusting and loyal behavior going forward.

Water should always be available, and it should be fresh. Don't cheat by just topping it up. Empty the bowl, scrub it clean and refill it every day.

Make sure her last meal of the day is a good two hours before bedtime so she's less likely to mess in the house during the night.

REMINDER
Never let her get hold of anything listed in the chapter:
'New puppy safety'

Manage toilet time

Remember that your puppy needs regular toilet breaks and it's up to you to help her with the when and where.

During the day, take her outside every hour if you can, or to the spot you'd most like her to use. When she does it there, make sure she understands that was a good thing by making a HUGE fuss of her. Give her a treat and tell her how spectacularly, amazingly brilliant she is.

At night, she won't want to go to the toilet in her special place but when she is very little she can only hold on for so long, so ideally you should be getting up during the night to take her out, as well as early each morning.

'But what about when she **does** mess inside?' you ask. What of it? She's a baby. Clean up well and be extremely patient. No matter what you've heard or read until now, don't punish her. She won't understand. (There's a whole chapter on toilet training coming up.)

Visit the vet

Vaccination regulations vary from country to country, so take her vaccination certificate with you and your vet

will advise you on what your puppy needs and when. Most vaccines require several rounds, between six weeks and 16 weeks, so scheme in the remainder of these during this first visit.

Be sure to tell the vet if you have plans to take your puppy to puppy classes or boarding kennels, because either of these require further inoculation.

Get advice on deworming, and the prevention of parasites.

If your puppy has not already been microchipped, you could have that done now. (In the UK this is required by law.)

If your puppy's baby nails are very long and catching on everything, you could ask the vet or a veterinary nurse to clip them for you, or to show you how to do it yourself.

Make the visit fun for your puppy by giving her praise and attention, staying by her side when she gets her shots, and telling her how good she is. Possibly take her for a walk or give her a treat afterwards to create a positive association.

Handle her

Your puppy needs to learn that she is safe with people, that they mean her no harm, and that she has no reason to fear them or react defensively.

She should start learning this straight away through lots of physical contact. Pet her and handle her: fondle her paws, move her legs, run your hand over her tail, feel her ears, touch her nose, gently examine her teeth, rub her tummy, groom her, bath her. Pick her up and carry her around, supporting her at the chest as well as under her bottom.

Play with her

Spend lots of time playing with her. And even if she is confined to your property until her last vaccinations have taken effect – encourage her to experience the world through different surfaces. Put her on floor tiles, wood, carpet, grass, sand, rock, soft cushions, paper and blankets. Let her get used to them all.

Give her quiet time

She needs some time on her own too so she can learn not to be anxious later on when you aren't there or able to play with her. (See 'Time alone' in the next chapter.) Shut her in her special place for anything between five and 15 minutes, once or even twice a day.

Loosen her collar and harness

If she wears a collar, check the fit every few days. She is growing fast and it'll need to be loosened regularly. You should be able to fit two fingers between the collar and her neck. Check the fit of her harness too. You should just be able to put two fingers between your puppy and the harness at any point.

Insurance

If you're planning on taking out pet insurance but haven't got around to it yet, do that now.

12. EMOTIONAL DEVELOPMENT

FRAGILE! HANDLE WITH CARE

The first weeks with your Yorkie puppy are the strongest bonding period you will have, so it's especially important that you give her lots of time and patience, and are ultra-sensitive to her feelings. Of course, you should always be sensitive to her feelings, but this is also the worst time for anything to frighten her. It is when she is most over-sensitive and when negative stimuli are the most likely to leave a lasting impression. For example, a loud electric storm when your puppy is all alone could lead to a lifelong fear of storms.

But this is also a time of opportunity. If she's already afraid of something, it's a good time to try to recondition her. For example, if she's afraid of brooms, show her that you're not afraid of them. Handle them gently in her presence without pressuring her in any way.

Yorkies are extremely tuned in to their humans' emotions – more so than most breeds – so show her that most experiences are harmless. When you are calm, relaxed and unafraid of something, she will soon learn that she can be too. And the more you expose her to the real world now, the more confidence she will have going forward.

SOCIALIZATION

In puppy-speak this means introducing her – now when she is still young – to as many people and animals of all shapes, colors and sizes as possible. It is the best way to help your puppy adjust to her new life in your world, and in fact, it is probably the most important thing you can do to raise a happy Yorkie. You will be able to teach her fancy dog tricks for years to come, but during these next few weeks it's vital that you get her out and about. Use the time well and don't let it slip by. As soon as her vaccinations have taken effect, visit friends and have friends to visit her. If puppy parties and puppy training are on offer in your area, take her along. (The chapter 'Stepping out' looks at how to do this safely and considerately.)

HABITUATION

This means exposing her – when she is still young – to as many new places and conditions as possible. In all fairness, you can't shut her indoors then expect her to behave normally around new people, places and things.

As soon as her vaccinations have taken effect, take her with you everywhere you can and let her explore. Let her discover different smells, surfaces, sounds and sights. Take her into a park, to the school gates, for a walk along a river, go to a sports match, go to the shops, paddle through puddles. Walk her over and under bridges. Let her see cars and trucks and trains and planes. Thunder, lightning and snow might be hard to arrange, but ideally let her experience different weather conditions too. Take her out at night and walk her in the rain.

Feeling safe

It is imperative
though that during
these new experiences
she feels safe as well as
having fun. Helping her to
feel at ease in new situations
will go a long way towards
helping her grow up to be a happy and well-adjusted
dog, so stay close by her side through these new
discoveries and don't let any of them frighten or over-
excite her. Going forward, she can only be properly
receptive to your training when she is feeling confident
and secure.

Here are some ideas to help with this.

- If you come across a potentially frightening
  situation – some big kids playing rough and tumble
  at the park for example – watch her closely for
  signs of discomfort. If she is hiding between your
  legs, or tucking her tail between her legs, you
  should back off and find a different route.

- Never put her under pressure to get close to anyone or anything.
- Be alert and sensitive to her feelings, so you will know when to approach and when to stay away. There are many signs which mean different things in different contexts. (See the chapter 'Puppy-People Translator').
- If you are not sure how she feels, avoid having a tight lead, so she knows she has a choice. If she is curious, approach from a distance. Let her look, listen and smell, gradually closing the distance as she is comfortable.
- If what she is afraid of presents a real threat, you could pick her up and let her watch from your arms.

Accidental noise

Don't forget about background noises that you are accustomed to but might well frighten your puppy.

- **TV, computer and radio:** Be especially alert to sounds from any of these. Dogs barking aggressively in a chase involving hounds, for example, could leave her terrified. Turn the sound down or off if she becomes alarmed – and before then if possible.
- **Tension in the house:** Keep a good vibe in the house. If she hears angry voices or senses a bad mood, she won't understand that it has nothing to do with her (whether it does or not).
- **Fireworks and thunder:** Close doors and windows, and muffle the sound with your own music or voices. Stay close to your puppy, showing her that you are not afraid.

SHIVERING AND SHAKING

If your puppy starts shaking, this must be addressed straight away. There needs to be a change of circumstance and it's your job to make it. It's possible she is shaking for no particular reason, but it is very likely one of these.

- **Cold:** Unlike other dog breeds with their warm double coats, Yorkies have fine human-like hair. On top of this, they have difficulty regulating their body temperatures, so they really do feel the cold. Warm her up immediately. If she is wet, dry her, keeping her warm as you do. Even if the air temperature seems perfectly warm to you, she could be cold. Dress her in a warm, comfortable Yorkie outfit – they're incredibly cute, but they're also there for good reason.

- **Fear:** If you think she could be afraid, change the circumstances. Hold her differently, put her down, take her away from the person, place or thing, or take it away from her, until the shaking subsides. If what is troubling her is something she will need to get used to at some stage, start introducing her to it slowly.

- **Excitement:** She could be shuddering with pure joy or anticipation. This is okay, as long as it's in short bursts.

- **Hypoglycemia:** An imbalance of sugars in the blood stream can also cause shaking. To avoid this, it's important that your puppy has enough meals in the day, ideally three. Some breeds can eventually be fed only once a day, but not a Yorkie or any dog from the Toy Group. And if you are making changes to your puppy's diet, they must be introduced very slowly. See the section on 'Feeding' in the next chapter.

If your puppy's shaking comes with weakness, dizziness or trouble walking, rub a drop of honey onto her gums and take her to the vet.

TIME ALONE

Dogs owners are increasingly aware of their dogs' need to be socialized and exposed to everything, and many go to great lengths to arrange this exposure. But just as many owners forget that being alone is one of these experiences. In fact giving your puppy time alone is giving her one of her most essential life skills.

Yorkies are companion dogs and don't like being alone, but most of them **have** to be at some time or another and the best way to minimize or even prevent separation anxiety at a later stage is to start leaving your puppy on her own now, just occasionally, during the day. If she is lucky enough to be right by your side for most of the time this is even more important.

Start practicing slowly.

- Choose a time when she is getting tired and likely to sleep soon.
- Take her out for a little play and a toilet break.
- Shut her in her crate or special place with everything she needs.
- Ignore any whining and leave the room or go out for a short while.
- If she is very little and goes to sleep while you are out, open the door or crate door when you return so she can get out when she wakes.
- Start off with about five to ten minutes and build it up slowly to no more than an hour while she's still

a puppy. For one thing, she will be needing the toilet.

There is a full chapter coming up on separation anxiety and how to prevent it.

BARKING

It's important not to punish barking during your puppy's first weeks in her new home, for all the reasons we've considered. She should be allowed to explore and to express herself.

If she's barking because she's worried about something, and you know her fear is unfounded, lead her away from it and give her a treat. Reassure her with a gentle voice, then gradually expose her to whatever it is that she is afraid of, showing her that you are with her, that you are not afraid and that there is nothing to worry about.

AGGRESSION

Your puppy might growl in play and ravage her toys when she is teething, but she is unlikely to show aggressive behavior now. That said, any dog can develop aggressive behavior in time, and an excellent way to prevent this is by handling your puppy lots and often while she is very young. Teach her now that you can hold and touch her, her toys and her food whenever and however you please. You are the leader and you are in charge.

How? By doing just that. Handle her, her toys and her food whenever and however you please. That way she is less likely to become territorial and possessive over what she considers to be her things.

SMALL CHILDREN

We've touched on this already – that small children need to be taught how to behave around your puppy, and fully supervised. Put yourself in her paws and imagine small children rolling around on the ground with you, giggling and shrieking, and how quickly that would encourage you to mouth and nip. Imagine being picked up continually, carried around, possibly even dropped, pestered, woken up. Think what it would be like not to be able to say, 'I don't want to play any more'.

NOTE
Puppies grow up fast compared with human children.
One week in your puppy's life is equivalent to around
five months' development in a human child.

FURTHER CRATE TRAINING

If you are using a crate and it started off at your bedside overnight, you should move it further from the bedroom – step by step if you like – to its permanent day-time position in the house. But only do this as your puppy grows in confidence and don't rush it. Your job is to build her trust.

If your puppy is going to be in the crate for a lengthy period while you are out, then you should leave her with some food as well as her water and toys.

EATING POO – SERIOUSLY?

Your puppy might eat poo – her own or another animal's. But don't panic. Revolting as it is, it's quite common in puppies. It's a difficult issue to address because nobody knows what it is that makes them do it. The good news is that they pretty much always grow out of it, and quite quickly too.

If you are faced with this problem, you might read or hear advice about upping her vitamin B content, but **never** give her human vitamins. Honestly, apart from sitting it out, the best things you can do are:

- clean up as soon as she's pooped
- keep her stocked up with interesting chew toys so she doesn't get bored
- keep her on a leash on walks so you can pull her away from other animals' poops
- if you have a cat litter box in the house, move it somewhere the cat can get to but she can't, for example the top of the washing machine.

LEADERSHIP

For her mental and emotional wellbeing, your puppy needs to see you, and all her human family, as her strong, clear leaders. Leading is never about punishment, but always about the clear communication that prevents bad behavior from developing in the first place. Clear communication leads to mutual understanding, and a better life for your puppy as well as everyone else in the family. This means that you, and every member of the family and household, must consistently use the same set of rules, spoken commands and body language.

It is also of utmost importance with a Yorkie not to be over-protective. Because these dogs are so well tuned to your feelings, if you are fearful of situations, she will quickly become nervous herself. Neurotic even.

The chapters 'Behavior' and 'Training' cover the key DOs and DON'Ts to help you build a strong foundation for a relationship based on understanding and respect.

EXERCISE AND PLAYTIME

These too are essential for your puppy's mental and emotional wellbeing. In the chapter on 'Exercise' we will look at how much and how often, and 'Stepping out' is full of advice and tips for safe and enjoyable outings.

Playing is also essential for a well-balanced, confident dog. It strengthens her relationship with you as well as improving her overall social interaction. In fact playtime is so important that there's a full chapter devoted to this too, with key pointers to help you make every game and every play session a positive experience.

13. ESSENTIAL CARE

When we think about a puppy's practical needs, we think food, shelter, hygiene, but we mightn't consider sleep. By around 12 weeks of age, your puppy will be needing 15-18 hours of rest or sleep a day, so make sure she has the quiet time she needs.

Her collar fitting is also easy to forget, but she is growing fast and it'll need to be loosened regularly. Check daily that it is not getting too tight.

FEEDING

When?

If your puppy had been on four feeds a day with the breeder, then between four and eight months you could cut this back to three times a day. Divide her daily food allowance (according to the instructions on the pack) into three portions instead of four and alter your schedule for regular feeding to, for example, 7am, 12.30pm and 6pm.

And remember to avoid feeding too close to your bedtime, so she's less likely to mess in the house or her crate during the night.

How? Feeding tips

- You, or her primary caretaker if it's someone else, should be the person who feeds her most often.

- Feed her the amount stipulated on the packaging in line with her weight and age, and no more.
- Occasionally feed her by hand over the few first days, or weeks even. It is a good reminder to her that you are the source of her food. It also prevents her from turning into a growler one day when she might feel her food is under threat.
- If you have more than one dog, feed them in different rooms, or in different corners of the same room and at least six feet apart.
- To prevent her from becoming a fussy eater, keep to mealtimes, but if she doesn't eat her food, don't leave it down all day. Take it away after 15 minutes, and don't feed her again until her next meal.
- Avoid feeding immediately before or after exercise.
- If you are eating around the same time as she is, make sure you eat first to remind her that you are at the top of the pecking order.

Change of food

You most likely started your puppy off on the diet she was having with her breeder, and it is just as likely that in time you will want to change her food. If you do, incorporate the new brand slowly. For example, in the first week give her one quarter of the daily allowance of the new food with three quarters of the daily allowance of the old. In the second week, make it half of one with half of the other. In week three increase the new food to three quarters; and in the fourth week it can make up the full meal.

What to feed

There's a baffling array of dog food brands and flavors on the market, so if you're making this decision without

the advice of the breeder or your vet, don't skimp –
with dog food you generally get what you pay for. And
don't buy more than one bag at a time so that if she's
lost interest in it by the end of the bag you can soon let
her try another brand. It's common for dogs to be
hugely enthusiastic about a particular food the first few
times they try it and then suddenly change their minds.
Mealtimes will always be high-points in her day, so it's
only right that you shop around for a food she loves.

- Make sure you choose a high-quality food that is
  appropriate for her breed.
- Make sure this food is also appropriate for her age
  – puppies need higher levels of both protein
  and fat in their diets than adult dogs.
  Many breeders recommend a high-
  quality premium dry puppy food.
- Avoid artificial coloring,
  sweeteners, sugars and salt.
- Don't overfeed. It is
  important not to let her get
  overweight at any stage of
  her life.

Some owners prefer to
feed their Yorkies home-
cooked meals. If you have
the time or inclination for
this, you will need to do
some research beyond
this book. Home-made
food can also be a
solution for Yorkies
that are fussy eaters
or suffer specific food
allergies.

Treats

Yorkies are not prone to weight gain. Nevertheless, treats should be counted into your puppy's daily food intake, making up no more than 10%. A safe way to ensure this is to pocket some dry food from her pre-measured daily allowance to use as treats and bribes during the day. You could also supplement her diet with carefully chosen chews and treats, but never feed these as scraps from the table.

Begging

Yes, those pleading eyes are near impossible to resist, but you absolutely have to be stronger than she is adorable. The best way to avoid begging is not to let it start in the first place. Never give in to her if she begs at the table, and never feed her from your plate. Make people-food off limits from day one, and if begging does become a problem at mealtimes, confine her to another room until it stops.

Eight months and older

Between eight and 12 months you can gradually transition your puppy's food to a 'junior' and then an 'adult' formula.

GROOMING

Even though Yorkies are low shedders, they need daily brushing so their hair doesn't become matted. They also need frequent washing, and because their coats grow throughout their lives, they need clipping too. All Yorkies need regular teeth cleaning, and most Yorkies need their nails trimmed from time to time.

Brushing

If brushing your dog's coat is something you enjoy, then brush as often as you like because this is not simply detangling and de-matting. It strengthens the bond between you; it keeps her skin healthy, her coat aerated and helps you to pick up on any lumps, sores or parasites. It is also very good for teaching her to be handled, especially during vet visits.

Start with a brush with soft bristles and brush in the direction of hair growth. Begin at the head, and work towards the tail and down the legs. Have short sessions to begin with in case she's getting restless.

It's normal for her to want to get the brush in her mouth at first, so be patient with her and don't give up because you think she doesn't like it. Build the time up slowly and she will soon grow to love these sessions.

Finish grooming by wiping her eyes with a warm, damp cloth. Wipe her ears too, but never go deeper than you can see.

Washing

Because your puppy's natural oils are keeping her skin and her coat healthy, avoid washing her too often, and certainly no more than once a week. You can use your own bath (ideally with a non-skid mat on the bottom), a washtub, or even the basin or a sink. If you're using a basin or sink, be extra careful not to let her wriggle out of your grasp.

- Get everything close to hand before you start. You will need a quality dog shampoo – never use people shampoo or conditioner, a sponge or cup, a soft brush, some treats and a small towel. And put on old clothes and a good sense of humor because you're likely to get wet.
- Lift your puppy carefully into the bath or tub, offering lots of praise and treats.
- Being careful to avoid her head and ears, run luke-warm water over her. This could be with a hand-held sprayer or a cup, or you could soak her with a wet sponge.
- Squeeze a drop of shampoo into your palm, smooth it onto her coat and lather (still being careful to avoid her head and ears) then rinse

several times, working the shampoo out with your hands.

- Last of all, clean her head and ears, including inside the ears, by wiping gently with a soft, moist cloth.
- Wrap her in a towel and rub her gently before lifting her out.
- When her coat is almost dry, it's an excellent time to give her a little brush.

Hair cuts

If your puppy's hair is growing long around the inside corners of her eyes, you should keep this trimmed. As well as helping her to see better, it will help keep the area clean. You can do this yourself, being very careful of course, with a pair of blunt-nosed scissors.

It's a good idea to invest in some clippers for trimming the long hairs in her ears. You can also use these to clip around the bottom and groin area to help keep her clean when she goes to the toilet.

After a few months, her coat will get longer, and the black hairs will gradually become bluer. Some owners choose to have the hair on their puppies' heads shaped and the coat shaved as early as four months old. But, even if you plan to keep her with a short puppy cut, she will only really need her first full-body trim between nine and 12 months.

There's a whole gamut of lengths and styles you can choose from for your adult Yorkie, but it would be sensible to take her to a professional groomer for these.

Nails

Your puppy's nails impact directly on how she walks, so they must be kept short. You might find that exercise on pavements and hard ground wears them down naturally, but any time they do get unmanageably long they will need to be trimmed. Vets and dog groomers can do this for you but if your puppy's nails need doing as often as every month or two, it would pay off in the long run to buy your own dog nail-trimming clippers – which are specially designed to prevent over-trimming – and learn to do it yourself.

Clipping is obviously not something you can practice every day, but what you can do often is help your puppy to get used to the idea. Choose times when she is already relaxed, then take hold of her paw and tap her nails gently with the clippers. When she responds calmly, praise her or give her a treat.

The next stage is to hold her paw, parting the hair away, and clasp the tip of a nail in the clippers – without making the clip but still showering her with praise when she stays calm. You might want to get someone to hold her for you when you do this.

When you are ready to make the cut you want to avoid the 'quick', which is inside the nail and contains sensitive nerve endings. Clip a tiny bit at a time – a millimeter or less – inspecting after each clip to make sure there is no bleeding.

If necessary, do no more than one or two nails at a time, praising her after each session, then making a note of the ones you've done.

If she has dewclaws – the nails on the upper, inner part of her feet – then don't forget to trim these too. (If she only has these on the front legs, or doesn't have any at all, don't worry. Some breeders will have had them removed soon after birth.)

When you've finished clipping, you might like to file the nails smooth with an emery board.

Do nail trimming often so that you won't have to cut much off at any one time, and soon your puppy will be comfortable with the process.

If clipping's not working out, you could try grinding the nails down with a dog nail-grinder instead.

Teeth

Yorkies are particularly prone to tooth decay and dental issues, so it is vital that your puppy has proper dental care from the moment you bring her home.

- **Home cleaning** – Ideally her teeth should be cleaned daily. But this should certainly be done no less than once a week.
  - Start by running your fingers across her teeth. Do this often while you are handling her, just as you might stroke her legs or rub her paws. Rub your finger along her teeth, being sure to touch all of them.
  - When she sits still and behaves, shower her with praise, treats and hugs.
  - After about a week with just your finger, begin using the dog finger toothbrush instead.
  - When she is managing this, add a small dab of dog toothpaste. (Never use human toothpaste.)
  - Give this a name, like 'toothbrush time', and she

will come to learn that this is when she must sit close to you and keep still.

- ◦ Build the length of the brushing time up to two to three minutes, making sure to clean all the teeth. In time you can also progress to a three-sided brush.

- **Professional cleaning** – While your home brushing will help to remove plaque, only scraping will remove tartar. This needs doing approximately every two years and is no easy task. You might want to try it yourself, and for that you would need to do further reading, but if not, your vet will certainly be able to help.

- **Bonus cleaning** – There are lots of treats on the market that double as dental chews to clean your puppy's teeth and keep her gums healthy. But don't use these instead of brushing.

- **Tooth watch** – From around five months old, you should begin keeping a close eye on the progress of your puppy's new adult teeth. Yorkies are prone to retaining their baby teeth and this can cause the adult teeth to push through unevenly. If you notice an adult tooth trying to push through while a baby tooth is still there, you should take her to the vet immediately.

Fleas and ticks

To prevent parasites, it's worth using a breed-specific, vet-recommended treatment, but never before she is 12 weeks old.

If your puppy does get fleas, wash her as usual, combing her while wet using a fine-toothed or flea comb. After each brush, rinse the comb in hot, soapy water. Then wash her bedding, and clean and vacuum the house thoroughly to get rid of any unhatched eggs.

If you find a tick, don't panic. It happens. But don't just pull it out either. Cover it with petroleum jelly which will suffocate it and force it to release its hold. Wait five minutes, then pluck it off using tweezers or your nails, from as close to the skin as possible to make sure the head doesn't stay behind.

Extra pampering

When your puppy is older, you might want to indulge her with some pampering treatments. There's a huge range of pet-safe products to choose from, from detangling conditioners and deodorizing sprays, to scented paw waxes and nose balms. And if you're a fashionista, a Yorkie never looks out of place suited and booted, and even be-ribboned. In fact, if the hair on the upper part of your Yorkie's head is not trimmed short, it should be pulled up into a topknot to avoid irritation. According to the AKC breed standard, it should be tied with one bow in the center, or parted in the middle and tied with two bows.

14. BEHAVIOR

Your puppy loves you so much! She wants to learn from you and please you. But she only knows what her survival instincts tell her, so, to reiterate, it's your job to teach her what is and isn't allowed in your world.

We will look at specific behaviors in the next chapters, but the pointers in this general chapter are fundamental to every one of them.

For a well-behaved Yorkie puppy, the first thing to understand – and I'm sure you do by now – is that puppies are much more receptive when they have nothing to fear. A fearful puppy will never be totally engaged.

Our understanding of animal behavior is improving all the time, and it's no longer acceptable to punish dogs, never mind puppies, by shouting, smacking and rubbing their noses in the carpet. This sort of treatment is both ineffective and counterproductive. It scares your puppy and puts you in a bad mood. You lose your dog's trust and the spinout of that – into all the other areas of the relationship – is just not worth thinking about. You want your puppy to be happy and optimistic, looking forward to everything, rather than fearing it.

So how do you achieve this? In a nutshell: you gain her trust by focusing on the things she does right. By encouraging good behavior and rewarding it.

Encourage and reward

Always tell her what you DO want her to do, rather than what you DON'T want her to do. If she's got the TV remote between her teeth, don't shout and get angry. Calmly distract her with something else, something she IS allowed to chew on. Refocus her onto this new and exciting treat or toy, and rescue the remote. If you don't have anything at hand, then ask her to do something to obey you – even something as simple as a 'Sit!'

Then, when she IS doing that something you DO want her to do, say 'Yes' or 'Good puppy' in a happy and positive voice. And if there's a treat at hand, treat her immediately.

> *TIP: If your treat-bribes start losing their appeal, look for better, tastier ones.*

Her feelings are everything

Let's say your Yorkie bounces up to you with a glint in her eye, a wiggle in her tail and a captured, disheveled designer t-shirt in her mouth. Try not to think about your favorite shirt which, after all, is just a thing and has no feelings at all. Instead, think about HOW SHE'S FEELING about what she's done. She thinks she's done brilliantly, doesn't she? She wants a medal. Scold her now and you'll really confuse her. Then again, if you praise her, she might keep bringing you t-shirt-type presents ad infinitum. So what do you do?

You don't scold or praise. Distract her instead by calling her to you and getting her attention onto something else, a toy perhaps. When she is refocused on the toy, offer her a tempting chew. By then the shirt should be far from her mind, and you should be able to rescue it. And if it's still wearable, remember to keep it up out of her puppy-jaw reach for a few months.

Prevent bad behavior

- Try to anticipate things that might go wrong. If you think she's about to chase the cat, hold on to her and distract her with a toy.
- Make sure her basic needs are met: love, food, water, warmth, things to chew on, sleep, play, exercise and exploration. If she has all of these she is far less likely to behave badly in the first place.
- Don't put temptation in her way. If you don't want her eating from your dinner plate, don't leave it lying around, unattended and in easy reach. That would just be setting her up to fail.

BUT don't molly-coddle

Through all this love, care and consideration, it's imperative that you don't spoil her. In the long run, going too easy on your Yorkie can be just as unfair as punishing her. And it would come back to bite you both because a Yorkie that is waited on hand and foot, over-protected and allowed to get away with bad behavior can become neurotic, possessive, territorial, fussy, a nipper, a nuisance barker … or any combination of these. While being gentle and loving, you must also be firm. Here's how.

Ignore her when you disapprove

In many bad behaviors, the best way to tell your puppy you don't like what she's doing is to take away something she wants – your attention. So the very best way to discourage bad behavior is by ignoring her when she's behaving in any way that is not acceptable to you. So:

- don't chase after her when she's taken something she shouldn't have.
- don't pick her up when she's whining or barking.
- don't yell at her when she doesn't come.
- don't push her off if she jumps up on you or others.

Ignore her, and make it as obvious as you can: stop playing, walk away, fold your arms, look away, even leave the room if you can.

You are the leader

To establish a positive relationship, your puppy must understand from the start that, even though you love her to the proverbial moon and back, your word is law and she must listen to you. And she will, as long as you are a worthy leader and a good teacher.

Here are some key tips and reminders.

- Be crystal clear in your instructions. Use single words rather than sentences and try to be consistent in your choice of words. Don't switch between 'Come!' and 'Here!' for example, or 'Walk!' and 'Heel!'.
- Keep your tone positive.
- Use body language as well as verbal commands.

- When she does what you want, show her unreservedly how clever she is. Be happy and excited and reward her with praise.

Rules must be consistent

I know, I know, we've been here before, but this is really important. If one person lets your puppy onto the sofa, it's downright unfair for someone else to reprimand her for being there. Rules will be very confusing if they differ from person to person, so it's really crucial that everyone in your puppy's life understands and teaches what is and what isn't allowed using the same set of rules, spoken commands and body language.

Timing is all-important

It's vital that you teach your puppy with timely signals – signals that apply to what she is doing AT THAT TIME. If you try to tell her off for something she did two minutes ago, she won't understand what she's done wrong. For example, if she runs off after a cat and then comes back, and you shout at her for chasing the cat as she is coming back, she will naturally think you are shouting at her for coming back and not for chasing the cat. The result? She is confused and intimidated, and next time she will think twice about coming back. Too many well-meaning dog owners make the mistake of misplaced timing – and it's simply unfair.

When to say 'No!' or 'Leave!'

There will be times when you absolutely do need to tell her her behavior is unacceptable. For example, if she is doing anything that could endanger her own life or cause harm to someone or something else. It also applies when she brazenly ignores your voice command because she would rather do something else.

These need to be corrected immediately and here's how.

- Reprimand her straight away. Say 'NO!' or 'LEAVE!' in your emergency voice – a voice that is so much louder and sharper than your usual quiet and calm voice, that it startles her enough to prevent or stop her behavior. Use this voice sparingly for best effect.
- Block her way with your body, or physically stop her if you need to.
- Then make eye contact and use your voice to get her to focus on you.

- Once you have her attention, praise her for changing her focus.
- 'No' and 'Leave' are never enough on their own because your puppy doesn't know what she's meant to do instead. Always try to give her something better to do or to chew on.

Still struggling?

If you've tried all these things with a bad behavior, using repeated, clear and consistent communication, and you're still struggling, you can resort to time-out. Shut her in the kitchen, or a similar and safe place (NOT her crate or special place), and leave her for a few minutes – five is acceptable, ten is too long.

Serious behavioral problems

These include incessant barking, aggression and destructive chewing. But all problems are caused by something, be it boredom, loneliness, lack of socialization, lack of training, fear, anxiety or insecurity, being spoilt or badly treated, or even just poor breeding.

With problems related to nipping, biting or growling, it is especially important that you are able to tell the difference between playfulness and aggression. See the chapter 'Puppy-People Translator' for clues on reading the signs. If your puppy develops any traits that could endanger herself, you, or any other person or their dog, you should get help from a professional in dog behavior. And the same goes for any other serious behavioral problem.

Let's look at the most common issues in some detail.

15. TOILET TRAINING

Yorkies are among the more difficult breeds to house-train. The long and short of it is that when your puppy goes to the toilet in an acceptable place, and as soon as she has finished her business, it's time to celebrate. Good puppy! Good puppy! Good puppy! That way you will teach her that doing her business, in that particular place, means AMAZING things will happen.

Where to go?

If you have a yard or garden, 'that particular' place will naturally be outside, but if you live in an upstairs apartment it's a different story. If you have a balcony you could teach her to go there, as long as you've dog-proofed any railings and made sure it's escape proof. Some dog owners with balconies invest in a patch of weather-resistant artificial lawn.

However, if there is no balcony, constantly carrying her up and down stairs, or taking the elevator, would be setting her up for failure. You'd be better off investing in an indoor dog potty, litter box or doggy bathroom.

Training

Remember, at first your puppy has no idea that the whole house is not one big public toilet. This is something you need to teach her – and with time and patience. Here are some key DOs and DON'Ts to help speed up the process.

Do

- When you bring your puppy home for the first time, give her a guided tour. The sooner she understands that all this space is living area, the sooner she will stop using it as a toilet.
- Take her outside (or to the place you've set up for her) every hour, and within 15 minutes of finishing a meal.
- Also take her there immediately if you spot any of these tell-tale signs:
  - Sniffing and circling the floor
  - Whining, crying or barking for no apparent reason
  - Pacing up and down
  - Looking towards or sitting at the door to the toilet area
  - Scratching the floor.
- Carry or lead her to the spot you'd like to encourage her to use.
- Then wait. And wait some more. Stay with her – come rain or shine – watching her all the time.
- You can spur her on with an encouraging command, like 'quickly now' or 'wee time'.
- Wait until she's completely finished before you reward her, or she might only do half her business.
- As soon as she's finished, shower her with praise.
- If you've waited more than ten minutes, take her inside and try again in another 20.

Don't

- Punish her for piddling or pooping inside. Punishing her for something she can't help and doesn't fully understand would only make her nervous and slow her progress.

- Leave her outside (or in a piddle spot) on her own. She will just turn her attention to getting back to you, and when she does get back, she will very likely still need to go.

Tips

- When she goes to the toilet in the house, thoroughly clean the place she's marked and use a pet-safe odor eliminator. This is because next time she goes to the toilet she's likely to choose somewhere she can already smell wee or poop. (If possible, limit your puppy's access to carpeted areas because they're more difficult to clean.)

- If she has messed inside but on a training mat or piece of newspaper, carry this outside (if you have a yard or garden) to where you'd like her to go in future, and weigh it down there with something heavy so it can't blow away. The smell will act as a signal to her to do her business there next time.
- Ideally avoid puppy pads – they can encourage messing in other soft places like the carpets.
- If you're taking her outside during the night just pick her up, take her out, put her where you want her to go and say 'wee time' or whatever words you've chosen. Don't talk to her or fuss over her and if she gets playful, ignore her or it will be difficult for her to settle back down.

- Yorkies have small bladders. If you have a safe, well-secured yard, a doggy door or pet flap in the door, is a good idea so she can let herself out as soon as she needs to go.
- If a doggy door's not an option, try fixing a service

bell to the floor, or hanging a bell on a string, at the door that leads outside. Jingle the bell whenever you take her out, and she should quickly learn to jingle it herself when she needs you to let her out.

- Yorkies can be fussy about rain, so if yours goes to the toilet outside, a covered potty area is a very good idea.

How long will toilet training take?

Progress obviously varies from puppy to puppy, but it's safe to assume yours will leave the odd surprise for you until she's around six months or even a year, and it could take even longer for her to be accident free. Be patient. Be consistent. Persevere. You will get there.

NOTES

Your puppy will never wee or poop to spite you. Some dogs make a little wee as a sign of submission, and some wee with excitement. These should never be punished!

•

Both sexes that are un-neutered can mark their territory by urinating, but if they do this inside it is not because of poor house-training. It stems from completely different urges.

16. CHEWING HOUSE AND HOME

*'Puppies are constantly inventing new ways to be bad.
It's fascinating. You come into a room they've been in and
see pieces of debris and try to figure out what you had that
was made from wicker or what had been stuffed with fluff'*
Julie Klam

All dogs chew, especially puppies. They don't have
hands, so chewing is how they explore and learn about
the world around them. They inspect everything they
can with their mouths and teeth.

They also chew because they are teething. By 12
weeks, your Yorkie's adult teeth, a full 42 of them, are
waiting to push out those super-sharp baby teeth. It
then takes until around 16 weeks for those baby teeth to
even start falling out, and the teething process goes on
until she is around eight months. Imagine her
frustration. That's a lot of weeks of important but
uncomfortable chewing to be done so – for the sake of

your puppy, your house and your sanity – keep valuables out of reach.

Your puppy will chew on anything she can during this time. Be understanding, and always have an abundant supply of toys and treats at hand that she IS allowed to chew on.

TEETHING TIPS

Tie a knot in an old cloth, wet it and put it in the freezer. Then give it to her when it is frozen to ease her sore gums.

Give her a piece of chilled or frozen carrot to chew on.

Don't

- Don't leave valuable and tempting chewables, like shoes, lying on the floor. Anything left lying around is fair game. Yorkies are excellent training for untidy owners.
- Don't leave supposedly-less-tempting chewables lying around either. Things like sunglasses, mobile phones and even car keys.
- Don't leave tempting loose ends within reach, like bits of wallpaper and dangling curtain ties.
- Don't encourage sticks. They can splinter and get stuck in her mouth.
- If you find your puppy chewing something small that she shouldn't have, an earplug for example, don't try to force it away from her. She might decide to swallow it instead of giving it back.
- And don't start a tug-of-war.

Do

- Instead of trying to pull or coax a forbidden item from your puppy, replace it with something she **is** allowed to chew on – and make sure this replacement offering is something you know she loves. As she plays with the forbidden item, hold the new and better offering to her nose and say, 'Leave!', 'Drop!' or 'Off!'.

- When she drops it, you can give her the treat and a pat.
- Make sure you have lots of puppy treats and toys. (Pet toys are created to appeal to your dog by smell, taste, feel and shape.)
- Keep these prizes close by. You never know when you'll be needing them.
- If you see your puppy approaching something with demolition on her mind, call her with a happy voice. Puppies are easily distracted, and she should immediately forget what she'd planned to do and come running to you. Reward her for coming and give her something more suitable to get her teeth into.
- If she's got a taste for something that can't be moved – a table leg for example, spray it with a pet-friendly anti-chew, or citronella.
- If you suspect she has eaten something harmful, call the vet immediately.

Chewing is an essential phase in every puppy's development, and her need to gnaw on everything in sight could carry on for months. Hang in there because it **will** lessen. It just won't happen overnight.

17. MOUTHING AND NIPPING

All Yorkies love play, and playing for all dogs involves mouthing one another, so it's completely natural for your puppy to want to play-bite. She might also bite because she's teething. It's possible that, like many new puppy owners, you don't mind her chewing your hands now, but you soon will. As she gets older, the biting will get harder and involve others too, so it's important that she learns as soon as possible not to use her teeth on people.

Adult dogs are good at controlling the pressure of their jaws, but puppies often make the mistake of biting too hard because they are still learning and practicing jaw control. If a puppy bites one of its litter mates too hard while playing, the hurt puppy will yelp and stop playing. Your puppy has already learned from its siblings that biting too hard inhibits play time.

She will learn gradually to play more gently until she understands not to let her teeth into contact with your skin at all.

Do

- Play with her with a chew toy in your hand. If she bites you and inflicts pain, make a high yelping sound and immediately withdraw your hand. This is exactly what would have happened with her litter mates, so it will help her to learn that it's okay to nip the chew toy, but not your hand.

- If the biting persists, remove yourself from the game, the room even, just for a few minutes to show her that teeth on skin equals no more playing. It's not a quick fix, but she will gradually make the association.
- Supervise small children. Their tendency when a puppy mouths them is to scream and run around, which only excites and encourages the puppy even more.

Don't

- Shout at her or smack her if she mouths or nips. This can make the biting harder to control.
- Rush her progress. She must learn jaw control gradually and through experience.
- Play rough tug games – they just encourage biting.

18. DIGGING – INSIDE AND OUT

Not all Yorkies dig, but many do, and the diggers among them will scratch at your floors, pull up your rugs and even rip up their all-time favorite ... your wall-to-wall carpets. Outside they will dig anywhere there is sand or gravel, or a small hole in the ground. They will rearrange your carefully tended flowerbeds and, more importantly, there is the possibility they could dig a hole under the fence and get out.

So what to do?

Outside the best solution is constant supervision. Ideally Yorkies should always be supervised outdoors for their own safety (because bobcats, coyotes, foxes and even birds of prey and other dogs are a risk). That way, if she starts to dig you can distract her, or move her away. But if she is ever likely to be outside without supervision:

- make sure your property is escape-proof. Walls or fences should be buried a good six inches under the ground. Alternatively chicken wire could be laid along the base.
- fence off newly planted flowerbeds.

Digging indoors, however, is more of a challenge so ask yourself why she might be digging, and here are some things you can try:

- If her digging might be due to boredom, you could try distraction. Give her other, more appealing sources of entertainment, like activity toys. (See the chapter' Playtime'.)

- Perhaps she wants something very specific. If she's digging persistently at a certain spot, and that spot is near some furniture, check under the furniture to make sure she's not simply trying to get at a toy that's rolled out of her reach.
- Maybe she's just using up excess energy. Try increasing her daily exercise with longer walks or playtimes.

Another way to address her digging instinct is to embrace it and make it fun.

- Inside, give her a pile of old clothing or fabric that she's allowed to dig around in. To get her started, bury a toy or treat underneath for her to find.
- Create a digging area outside that's just for her. Invest in a sand box where she can dig to her heart's content.

Preventative measures

- If it's possible, restrict her access to the areas she targets.
- If it's not possible, try an anti-chew spray like apple-bitter or citronella on these areas.
- Keep her nails short, and even smoothed with a nail file, to minimize the damage.

Desperate measures

- If she persists in digging where she shouldn't, make an unpleasant clanging noise. Rattle some coins in a tin or hit a pot with a metal spoon until she associates her digging in that place with this horrible noise.

19. BARKING

Yes, Yorkies bark. They can be extremely vocal. Your puppy will bark for very good reason, no reason at all, just for fun, to make suggestions and even to make demands. In fact, she will have a whole box-full of bark tricks, each with their own distinct meaning, and you'll soon learn the difference between them.

Barking at others

Yorkies make excellent watch dogs – you'll certainly never need a doorbell. It's natural for them to warn you about strangers or intruders, and that kind of barking is not necessarily something you want to stop or even discourage. Let your puppy bark, momentarily at least, then call her back to you and praise her, or distract her with a toy or a treat if you need to.

If she doesn't stop barking then, as with pretty much all bad behavior, it's most effective to give her the 'I'm ignoring you now!' treatment.

- Don't shout at her. If you shout at her while she's barking, she's likely to interpret your shouting as 'people barking', and think you're egging her on, or even coming to help. The result? She will bark even harder.
- Don't talk to her or touch her
- Instead, turn away from her
- Leave the room or area if you can

- If she won't stop barking and it's becoming a problem, you could distract her with a loud noise (like shaking some coins in a tin can)
- Then, as soon as she has settled down, acknowledge and reward her for her new-found quiet behavior.

Barking at you

As your puppy comes to see that her efforts to win your attention, like jumping up or nipping, are fruitless, she might well replace these with her latest greatest trick – a demanding yap that says: 'I am still here', 'Stop ignoring me', 'Hey, I want some of that too' or 'Come on, let's play.'

Whatever it is, she wants your attention. Don't give it to her. Instead, pull out your now-well-practiced ignoring techniques.

Barking to communicate a need

The exception is a genuine plea. For example, if something is truly scaring her, or she wants to go outside for the toilet. Consider her body language in the context of whatever else is going on around her, and you will soon learn which barks are attention-seeking and which express a real need or genuine fear.

Incessant barking

This can become a real issue for Yorkie owners, especially if they share their space with others or live close to their neighbors.

But problem barking is seldom without reason. For example, if she is left on her own for long periods, shut in a small space, or trying not to relieve herself inside, she WILL bark. And who could blame her? Even a mature Yorkie would do that.

Where the barking is linked to a genuine need, it is the need that needs addressing, rather than the barking, so try to find out what's setting her off in the first place. The most common causes are loneliness, frustration, boredom or lack of attention, and here are some things you could try.

Do

- Make sure she isn't barking because she feels threatened by anything.
- Move her to a less isolated place.
- Arrange for there to be more space for her to play in.
- Leave more toys for her to play with.
- Take her for longer walks.
- Give her more time to interact with you and other dogs.
- If she's alone during the day, arrange for someone to come and walk her or play with her.
- If she's likely to be left alone for long stretches, consider getting another dog for company.

Don't

- Leave your puppy alone for a long time. It's simply not fair.

Getting serious

If you've been consistent, persistent and patient with her training and she is still barking incessantly and for no apparent reason, you might need extra help. There are methods and products you can try and buy, but most of them punish barking rather than reinforcing positive behavior, so it would be better in the long run to consult a dog behavior expert who can come to your home.

20. SEPARATION ANXIETY

This is the fear of being alone.

It's inevitable that you will need to leave your puppy alone at times, even for very short stretches. But for a Yorkshire Terrier, being away from you, the center of her world, is a very real cause of stress and arguably the most serious problem faced by the breed today. Yorkies that are left alone for long stretches can easily suffer depression and anxiety as a result, and this shows itself in negative behaviors including: barking, whining, pacing, self-licking, destructive chewing, drooling and even loss of bowel and bladder control.

Your puppy will quickly learn the indications that you are going out – like putting on your shoes, fetching your bag or picking up the keys – and the anxiety will start to kick in as soon as she picks up on these signs.

She won't want you to leave, so she'll most likely start following you, jumping up on you and seeking your attention in any way she can. Never punish her for showing signs of distress at your leaving. She's not being naughty. Being such fabulous companion dogs makes Yorkies more prone to separation anxiety than most breeds. And this makes it all the more important that you manage leaving her with care and planning.

First steps

Do your leaving-the-house things often and from day one, like picking up your keys, and walking outside and coming straight back in again.

It is wise to start leaving her on her own from early on – within the first few days and for just a few minutes a day – so she understands quickly that this is normal and there is nothing to worry about. But before actually leaving her for the first time, make sure she's had time to really bond with you.

- Create a small but special place to leave her, her crate or a playpen for example, and fill it with everything she needs: bedding, water, food, wee mat. This small den-like space will keep her feeling safe, and really is preferable to letting her roam around the house, which can actually make her feel exposed and more alone.
- Then include distraction toys or treats – ones that can double as separation anxiety aids. There's a

remarkable range of products to choose from, including:

- toys filled with slow-release treats
- interactive toys that respond to touch with squeaking or even speaking
- companion toys – stuffed animal toys that mimic the heartbeat and body warmth of another dog
- pet cams which enable you to monitor your puppy and even flick her treats via an app on your smartphone.

Another advantage of the enclosed space is that it keeps these items close by.

- Choose a time when she's getting tired and likely to sleep soon, after a walk or an exciting playtime for example.
- Take her for a toilet break.
- Put her in her 'den', ignore any whining and leave the room or go out for a short while (five to ten minutes).
- When you get back, don't make an unusually big fuss of her.
- If she is asleep when you return, open the crate door or puppy gate so she can get out when she wakes.

Lengthening the separation

- When you start leaving her for longer periods, do it very, very gradually, building up to no more than an hour until she is around six months. For one thing, she will be needing the toilet.
- If there are other members of your household, make sure they spend time with her too so she doesn't become overly dependent on one person. They should also feed her, walk her, play with her and handle her.

- Never punish her for signs of anxiety when you're leaving, or for having misbehaved while you were out.

  TIP: *Don't make a big fuss of her when you leave or get back home. Be as matter of fact about it as you can.*

Leaving her for a long time

Ideally don't do it. But there could be times when you are left with no choice. Here are some ideas to minimize the stress.

- Drop her off with a responsible family member, friend or dog-sitter.
- Ask a neighbor or pay a pet-sitter to come and spend some time with her.
- Employ a dog walker.
- Take her for a decent walk before you set off. Exercise has a calming effect, and she'll be more likely to have a sleep when you leave.
- Make sure she has everything she needs, including fresh water and plenty of toys.
- Consider the changes in temperature of her special place while you're out. You might've left her with a lovely window view which, later in the day could leave her confined in glaring sunlight. Perhaps the air conditioning is set to come on while you are out, or the heating will soon go off. Yorkies are highly sensitive to both heat and cold, so she should always be in a comfortable room temperature.
- You could leave soothing music playing in the house. Some soundtracks are created specifically for keeping dogs calm and comforted.
- If it is likely to be dark when you get home, leave a light on.

21. EXERCISE

Yorkies don't need huge amounts of exercise, but giving your puppy the exercise she does need is an essential part of her care. It will keep her happy, healthy and stimulated, and prevent her from becoming bored, frustrated or hyperactive.

How much?

While your puppy is growing, her bones and joints are still firming up so her exercise should be limited. The recommended amount is five minutes per day per month of age, so on this basis:

- by four months she should be getting a total of 20 minutes' exercise a day. But ideally break this up into two ten-minutes sessions.
- by six months she should be getting a total of 30 minutes a day, but again, break this up. Three sessions of ten minutes each is ideal, but two sessions lasting 15 minutes is also fine if that works better for you.

- by nine months to a year, and as an adult, she should be getting a good 45 minutes' to an hour's exercise a day. If, with that, you find she is bored, destructive or putting on weight, you can increase the amount.

Walking

Try to take her on two short walks a day, ideally one in the morning and one in the evening. These can start as soon as her inoculations have taken effect, and there are plenty of tips in the next chapter.

Playing

As well as walking out, your puppy will need some cardio-exercise – short, intense bursts of activity to keep her fit and healthy. Playtime with exercises like racing after a ball are perfect for this and also count towards her daily activity. So if she is needing 30 minutes' exercise a day, for example, you could take her on two ten-minute walks and have ten minutes of high-energy playtime. Or, if you could only manage one walk, you could spend the rest of her allocated exercise time playing games like fetch. The chapter 'Playtime' is filled with ideas that are fantastic for physical as well as mental stimulation.

Swimming

If you live in a hot climate, swimming can be a great way for your puppy to exercise, while cooling off at the same time. Your Yorkie might not want to swim, and that's fine. Never make her. But there's every chance she might become a keen little swimmer, so if you'd like to give her the opportunity, here are some tips to help you keep the experience safe as well as fun.

- First and most importantly, any swimming must be under strict supervision.
- If you can, start with a kiddie pool and just two to three inches of water. Or take her to a place where the water deepens very gradually. Then entice her in using squeaky toys if she needs extra encouragement.
- Wherever it is, the water must be at least 78°F (25.5°C).
- If the water is deep, like a swimming pool, ease her in gently, staying physically close, and being acutely aware her feelings.
- You could put her in a life-vest, and it's worth investing in one with a grip handle on the top.
- On hot days, her skin will burn in the heat just like yours, even in the water, so spray her with a pet protector sunscreen.
- Take the same precautions with her as you would with a very young child, even if the water is shallow, and even if she is wearing a life jacket.
- Rinse her well after swimming, whether she's been in a pool, a lake or any other body of water.

When to exercise

Avoid exercising immediately before or after eating, or within an hour of her bedtime.

Yorkies thrive on routine, so choose her exercise and playtimes and stick to them as closely as possible.

Exercising responsibly

- Always supervise her closely when she's playing around children and other dogs.
- To protect her leg joints going forward,

remember to limit jumping from heights. Lift her over high obstacles when you're out walking.

- Also limit climbing up and down flights of stairs.
- And until she is fully grown, she shouldn't be going on any long walks.

22. STEPPING OUT

Once your puppy has had all her vaccinations, and you have waited another two weeks for them to take full effect, you can start taking her out. Of course you can carry her for all or part of your outings in the sling, backpack or pet carrier bag you have chosen for her, or even push her along in a pet stroller, but let's have a look here at the times when she is walking on her own four paws.

Eventually you want her to trot along at your side on a loose lead, but for a puppy, with seemingly endless stores of pent-up energy, this can be surprisingly difficult to learn. Start off practicing walking on the lead at home, and while you're waiting for her vaccinations to take effect is the ideal time.

Do

- Use a harness (not a collar) and a non-extendable lead.

- Attach the lead to the harness clip when she is calm and not resisting you.
- Start by letting her wander around the house with the lead trailing behind her, but try not to let her chew it.
- The next stage is to pick up the lead and encourage her to walk along beside you.
- When she is walking nicely alongside you, with the lead slack but off the ground, reward her generously with praise and treats.

Don't

- Connect the lead to her collar. That could put too much pressure on her neck.
- Drag her. That would only make her panic and pull away.
- If she is pulling, don't pull back, yank on the lead, or shout at her. Instead, stop and call her to you. Praise her when she comes, then try again.

When your puppy is ready for her first walks out, you'll want to introduce her to the big, wide world gently and slowly. These are a few things to consider and be aware of.

Safety

Think carefully about where you're going to take her and when, so you can avoid frightening or stressful experiences.

- Choose a safe, open space away from busy

roads, and where other dog owners are likely to act in a responsible way.

- Think about the best time to go. Perhaps it's too soon for a Saturday morning at the park if there is likely to be a noisy sports match in play.

What to take

As well as your puppy in her harness and the non-extendable lead, you will need:

- Poo bags – more than one
- Treats (ideally in a treat pouch) – so you can reward good behavior
- Water and a bowl. (As a space saver, you might like to invest in a pets' water bottle with a flap or lid that doubles as a bowl.)

Out and about

- Don't walk too fast for her. She shouldn't get out of breath trying to keep up with you.
- Stop often to pat her and talk to her.
- Give her time to sniff at things. She will love exploring new scents.
- If she poops, pick it up with a poo bag and dispose of it at home (or in a public dog waste bin if one is provided).
  - Use this time to practice good behaviors and commands.
  - If something scares her, let her know you are with her, protecting her, and that she is safe. Resist picking her up unless it is a real threat.
- She will most likely be loving the whole experience, but if she sits down and refuses to budge, don't put up with this. Just pick her up and carry on walking in your chosen direction.

Don't pick her up every time something scares her, or she will start thinking the world is too dangerous to walk about in.

Weather

The weather will play a big role in your puppy's enjoyment of the outdoors, so start your outings on days, and at times, that are as moderate as possible.

- **Heat** – Heat stress and heat stroke are real dangers for Yorkies, so outings on hot summer days must be taken with extra care.
  - Schedule your walks to avoid the hottest times of the day.
  - If you are taking the car, cool it down before you put her in.
  - Always take water. You can use it to help keep her cool as well as hydrated.
  - Consider your route and take the shadier, cooler paths.
  - Make plenty of stops for rest and water.
  - Apply a canine sunblock or sunscreen spray (never a human sunblock).
  - If the ground is likely to be hot, apply wax to her paws.
- **Cold** – Yorkies lose body heat faster than bigger dogs, and most smaller breeds too because of their fine hair, so outdoors on a cold day, your puppy must always be kept warm.
  - Dress her appropriately. If the air is cool, a light sweater could be best. For harsh winter cold, she'd need a thick coat and possibly a hat too. And if it is likely to be wet as well, then this warm clothing should be waterproof too.

◦ You also need to be mindful of her paws if she is likely to be walking on cold or icy surfaces. Apply a good paw wax, or put her in dog boots. Footwear can be fiddly and take a bit of getting used to, for both of you frankly, but if boots have a velcro fastening at the back, they should stay on without being uncomfortably tight.

Barking

Your puppy might well decide to bark at things and happenings along the way, and this is quite common in Yorkies. If she does, don't even slow down for a look. Just keep walking as if you're taking no notice. As she becomes accustomed to all these new things around her, she should stop barking at them, and when she does, reward her immediately with a treat and praise while still walking on.

Other dogs

If your puppy barks at another dog, however, possibly lunging towards it too, she most likely wants to interact. You want to nip this behavior in the bud, so rather than pulling her away or walking on, you could use the opportunity to practice her meeting and greeting. Often, simply being able to sniff a 'hello' at the passing dog is enough to diffuse her excitement.

But **never** assume that another dog walker or their dog are happy to reciprocate. Their dog might be injured and in recovery; not good with puppies or small dogs; or the owner could be working on a training exercise. Always ask first and from a distance:

1. whether their dog is good with puppies and

2. whether they are happy for your puppy to say 'hello'.

If it is okay for your dogs to meet, supervise closely so you can pre-empt any bad experiences.

- If there are any signs of aggression, pull her back quickly.
- Make sure you walk on past some dogs, and people too, so your puppy doesn't take it for granted that she can run up to anyone for a chin- and tail-wag.

Play dates

If your puppy meets another small dog she plays especially well with, you could arrange play dates at times that suit you both.

Together time

Put your phone out of temptation's way and make this time with your puppy real quality time.

Risks going forward

Walking out comes with its own risks – some obvious and others totally unpredictable, so it's advisable to keep your puppy, and even full-grown Yorkie, on a lead at all times. Even so, beware of other animals, dogs included, and be careful what she might find to eat, for example tasty plants that mightn't be safe.

With Yorkies the trick is to give her as much freedom and independence as you can, while always keeping an eagle-eye out for possible dangers.

23. TRAINING

'Properly trained, a man can
be dog's best friend'
Corey Ford

You probably think puppy training is about training your puppy – most people do – but in fact it is nearly all about you, learning how to communicate effectively with your newest member of the family.

You are going to need shed-loads of patience and perseverance because – while there's no doubt Yorkies are bright little buttons and quick to learn – their terrier independence and strong opinions can make them a handful to train.

If you find yourself feeling frustrated, you'll need to take yourself away, pull yourself together, and come back to it when you are calm. Because training absolutely **MUST** be positive, reward-based and nurturing.

In fact, everything from the chapter on Behavior applies to this chapter too because the premise for training is the same – that your puppy is more engaged when she has nothing to fear. You should train by encouraging and rewarding good behavior – always telling her what you DO want her to do, rather than what you DON'T want her to do.

And training can and should be fun. The best

trained dogs wag their tails during training because they are loving the challenge as well as the reward.

This is all about improved communication and understanding, so think of every minute as an investment in a better quality of life for you, your puppy … and everyone she meets.

Reward-based training

Praise is always a motivator in training, but with Yorkies you really do need to use food-based motivation as well, especially at first. When she does something right, reward her immediately with a

tempting treat, praising her at the same time with 'Yes' or 'Good dog' in a happy, encouraging voice.

In time, you can wean her from the food-based training and she will obey you purely for the fun of the training itself. But even then, reward her with treats intermittently.

When to start

Training starts the moment you bring your puppy home. Even if you've signed up for puppy classes at some future date, don't wait. Teach her what you can, little by little, moment by moment. When she's under six months, keep training to no more than ten minutes per session. Practice often, and never give up.

Who's responsible

Everyone in your puppy's close and extended family – and all using the same set of rules, spoken commands, hand signals and body language. No matter what training method you choose, consistency is the key.

Where?

Start training in a quiet place with no outside distractions. A closed room is infinitely better than a park filled with people, other dogs and interesting smells.

What needs to be learned?

By the time she is six months, your puppy should know her name and obey your orders to: 'Come', 'Sit' and 'Down'. She should also have been introduced to 'Stay'.

How?

All commands should be spoken clearly, firmly and with confidence. Lengthen the vowel sounds and make sure the consonants are crisp and clear.

Your voice and treats are key to training your puppy, but don't forget gestures. It might surprise you to learn that most puppies actually respond better to body language than words.

NAME RECOGNITION

One of the first things your puppy needs to learn is to recognize her name. After all, how else will she know that you're communicating with her?

Do

- From a short distance – three or four feet is fine – call her clearly, using her name just once.
- Use a happy, friendly voice.
- Crouch down if you can.
- Open your arms to welcome her (body language is hugely important).
- Make a fuss of her when she gets to you.
- If she doesn't respond, wait a few seconds then call again, still clearly, and still just the once.
- When she does come, praise her lovingly, give her a treat and tell her how brilliantly clever she is.
- Practice this often.

Don't

- Overuse her name or say it repeatedly in quick succession, or she will soon learn to ignore it.

EYE CONTACT

If your puppy is not looking at you, she is probably not listening either. Calling her name will encourage her to look at you and, when she does, you can know she's engaged. She's turning to you to find out what's coming next: will you open the door, take her for a walk, throw a toy? It's excellent that she's turning to you for answers and provision, so make sure you reward her.

CALLING TO YOU

If your puppy only knows one command it should be 'Come' or 'Here'. Coming to you when she's called is important for your relationship, and for her safety too. Recall is much like the name recognition exercise and now, while she is little, is a very good time to teach it to her because this is when she needs you more than ever for love, food and safety. In fact, if she's already joined your family, chances are she is with you right now, under your feet or helping you to absorb this book. Quite literally. And chances are she already relates the recall command to something fun and exciting: food, a new toy or play time.

Do

- Follow the steps in the Name Recognition exercise above, using her name and adding a calling word like 'Come' or 'Here'. Consistency is key, so choose whichever word you prefer and stick with it.
- Call her to you often, gradually increasing the initial distance between you.
- If she keeps following you anyway, find someone who can help you by holding her while you back away. Then entice her, if necessary, and when she is struggling to get to you, your helper can let her go. Only then, when she is running to you, call her name and 'Come' or 'Here'.
- Try getting down on your haunches or your knees and opening your arms wide to greet her.

Don't

- If you call your puppy to you and she gets side-tracked en route, you might be tempted to speak to her in a harsh voice when she finally does come back to you. Don't. Because if you do that, she'll only associate your harshness with the last thing she's done – come to you. Coming to you should ALWAYS be associated with good things. (See 'Timing is all-important' in the chapter on Behavior.)

'SIT'

This is one of the most useful exercises you can teach your puppy.

- Call her to you and hold a treat, palm facing down, just in front of her nose for her to smell.
- When you've got her interest, slowly take the treat up a couple of inches and over her head (slightly behind and above her eyes).
- When she lowers her bottom, and only then, say 'Sit!' and give her the treat.
- Once she is doing this well, you can move on to the next stage. Wait until her bottom is actually on the floor before you say 'Sit!', and then treat her.
- She will soon learn to associate the word with the action. In time she will sit after you've given the command, and you can teach her to sit for longer stretches and from further away.

'DOWN'

- It is best to start teaching this command when your puppy is already in an attentive Sit. You might also prefer to kneel in front of her rather than stand.

- Without feeding her the treat in your hand, move your hand, still palm down, from above her nose and towards the floor, between her front paws and close to her body.
- When she lowers her nose and front paws, keeping her bottom on the ground, say 'Down!' in a clear voice and give her the treat.
- When she is doing this well, you can wait until her tummy and all four paws are flat on the floor before you say 'Down!', and only then give her the treat.

'STAY'

This is an essential command for your puppy's safety –
or that of any dog that might dash out the front door,
across a road, or leap out of the car. The training
involves teaching her to stay in a Sit or Down position
for increasingly long times before you reward her.

- Once she is in a 'Sit' or a 'Down', say 'Stay!' in a
  strong but soothing voice, and combine this with a
  clear hand signal. Point to the ground just in front
  of her with your arm straight, your palm flat and
  your fingers together.
- If she gets up, simply ask for the Sit or Down
  position again and repeat the 'Stay' command.
- When she has stayed for a few seconds, say 'Good!'
  (or another 'release' word of your choice) and give
  her a treat.
- Gradually work up to longer times, but no more
  than 30 seconds, and step back in increments to
  increase the distance. (Try not to give her
  unrealistic goals; the idea is to push her to the limit
  while letting her succeed.)
- Keep her on a lead when you put this command
  into practice at the front door or in the car.

What if the training's 'not working'?

If your puppy doesn't do what you've asked (assuming
she has no difficulty with hearing):

- she doesn't understand and needs clearer
  instructions,
- she needs more practice,
- or she needs a better reason to obey you – like a
  treat, an even better treat (squares of fresh chicken
  or liver. Yum!), or higher praise.

EXPANDING ON THE BASICS

Extension exercises

- **Duration** – Once your puppy can do an exercise, like 'Sit' for example, you can gradually ask her to sit for longer periods before treating her.
- **Distractions** – You can slowly increase the distractions too. A 'Sit' when a squirrel is taunting your puppy from a nearby tree is very different from a 'Sit' in a quiet place. Once she's mastered the instruction in a quiet room, start practicing it in a busier part of the house, then at the park, and so on.
- **Distance** – In time, you can also begin asking your puppy to 'Sit' from slightly further away from you, but start with just a couple of steps and don't forget the all-important hand signals.
- **Advanced commands** – If you'd like to add to these basic commands, your puppy can go on to learn 'Settle', 'Heel' and many more. There are some excellent obedience training guides on the market.
- **Obedience training classes** – Alternatively, if training classes are available in your area they are well worth the effort, but look for a group that caters for small and Toy breeds, or has a high percentage of small dogs registered for the class.

TRICKS

There are lots of tricks you can teach your Yorkie, but start with one easy one and build on from there.

For example, you might like to teach her to give you her paw. Kneel down facing her, and have her in a Sit.

Say 'Paw' and hold out your hand to her. Just like you, she is either left or right pawed so she'll usually lift the same paw. Figure out which paw it is so you can ask her for her more natural gestures.

Another fun Yorkie trick is rolling over. Say 'Roll over' moving your hand in small circles in front of her nose in the direction she should roll. She will also have a best roll side, so learn which one it is and ask for that.

Practice one trick at a time. When she's mastered that you can move on to the next one. And if there's a trick or two she struggles to grasp, don't worry. Rather find ones she does understand. There are plenty of videos on the internet that can give you ideas for new tricks to try.

With both tricks and training, you're already halfway there because of your Yorkie's huge love for you and her eagerness to please. For your part, bring encouragement and effusive praise. Be consistent. Be patient. Persevere.

OTHER ACTIVITIES

Don't assume that because your Yorkie is small, she can't participate in obedience training or agility classes, or work with you in a therapy role. She absolutely can.

24. PLAYTIME!

Playing with your puppy is great fun. It also helps to develop her socializing, improve her communication skills, and give her the mental and physical exercise she needs. But whether this play is purely for fun or a structured exercise, keep these Rules top of mind.

- Start playtimes when your puppy is being good, so you're not rewarding her for bad behavior.
- Several short play sessions spread throughout the day are always better than one long one.
- Whatever games you're playing, remember she's only little, so be gentle, aiming to match your strength, speed and energy to her own.
- As far as possible, get down low to her level.
- If a toy is involved, avoid hard tugging – it puts too much pressure on her teeth and also encourages more aggressive play. A good way to manage the pressure is to hold the toy by your fingertips.
- When your puppy wins the toy, encourage her back to teach her that playing is more about having fun together than possession.
- If the playing does shift from fun interaction to possession of a toy, then stop for a while.
- Always try to calm the playing down before you stop. It's disappointing stopping a game when it's at its most exciting.

- And always end playtime on a good note. If you've had to stop for a moment, restart the game and end it when things are quiet and friendly.
- Avoid exciting games just before her bedtime.

For playtime to be great fun, you really just need each other – there's no need for fancy toys or expensive equipment. Sharing a walk or a paddle in a puddle can be the most special times. But if you're still looking to expand your activities, here are some ideas.

GAMES

Yorkies adore games that cater to their instinct to sniff, find and chase. Your puppy will have her own personal favorites and you'll soon figure out what they are.

Chase

This is excellent practice for encouraging your puppy to come to you when she is older.

1. Flick a treat across the floor.
2. Let her chase after it.
3. When she comes back for more, make eye contact and praise her.
4. Only then flick another treat across the floor, and so on.

Fetch

This is an extension of Chase, and requires a bit more space.

1. Throw things for her to fetch: toys, a ball, a treat.
2. Say 'Fetch!' as you throw each item.
3. Once she knows to fetch, start throwing the objects into harder-to-reach places.
4. If this doesn't work, throw more interesting toys or tastier treats.

Which hand?

1. With your hands behind your back, put a small treat or two in one hand and nothing in the other.
2. Make your hands into fists and bring them in front of you.
3. Let your puppy choose which fist she prefers the smell of.

4. When she's decided which hand she's interested in, and it's the right one, say 'Good!' and open your hand, letting her take the treat.

Which cup?

Using three or four cups or egg cups, place a treat under one of them and let her sniff it out. Next time, hide the treat under a different cup.

Treasure hunt

Your puppy will love rooting around for hidden treasure.

1. The first time you play this, let her watch as you hide a treat (something she can eat), then lead her away and say 'Find'. A good place would be under a piece of fabric she's allowed to dig around in.

2. Once she understands how the game works, you can make sure she can't see you when you hide the treat or a toy. Then lead her into the room or area where it's hidden, say 'Find', and this time she will have to sniff it out. (The first few times you might need to guide her.)

One day, when she is older and fully understands the game, you can make it more difficult by using 'Sit!' and 'Stay!' while you hide the treat, and then by hiding it in more difficult places too.

Obstacle course

1. Turn your passageway or living area into an obstacle course – make tunnels, fill a tea tray with water, arrange boxes or bottles to navigate around … anything you can think of that is safe.

2. Guide your puppy through the course and reward her with treats each time she overcomes an obstacle.

TOYS

Choose a range of toys with some that roll, bounce or squeak, and others that are simply soft and cuddly. But avoid anything with soft plastic that could be shredded into small pieces she might swallow.

To keep her interested in her toys, don't put them all out at the same time. Only let her play with or chew a few at a time, and rotate them through the week, or even the day.

If you're looking for toys to make playtime a little more interesting and challenging, here are a few ideas.

The maze

There are a number of 'slow feeder' pet toys on the market which are maze-like in design. These were originally intended for dogs who gulp their food down too fast, but they also work brilliantly for brain-training.

- Put a treat or two in the middle of the maze and let her use her paws, nose and tongue to work them out before she can eat them. (Make sure you've chosen one for small breeds so she can actually manage this.)

The hollow chew

Hollow toys made of hard rubber are available online and from most pet stores. The Kong is a great example; it comes in a range of sizes and is dishwasher safe. Fill one of these with small dog treats, or even with meat, carrot, marmite, banana or peanut butter (as long as it contains no Xylitol). Your puppy will spend hours trying to extract whatever you've filled it up with.

Treat-dispensing balls

Yorkies love balls, especially small squeaky ones, and generally speaking you should look for nice soft ones for the wellbeing of both your puppy and your house. A hollow treat-dispensing 'ball', however, is unlikely to be soft, and it mightn't be round, but no matter because it's not for throwing about. Instead your puppy will roll it around for hours trying to get the treat pieces out.

EQUIPMENT

Children's toy stores have some great products that would appeal to puppies just as much as to children – tunnels, playhouses, sand boxes and paddling pools for example. Use your imagination, making sure whatever you come up with is safe and well secured.

25. TRAVELING

Yorkies make excellent travel companions because of their temperaments as well as their size. What's more, they're usually permitted to travel with you whether you're going by coach, bus, train, subway, underground, cab, taxi, ship or plane.

BUT … this depends entirely on the transport provider because each one has its own rulings. For example, some flight operators will allow your dog on flights to some of its destinations but not to others. So it's always best to check when making your arrangements.

Many transport providers will allow you to carry your Yorkie onboard with you, but again each has its own guidelines on how your dog can travel. Most will insist on her being in an enclosed pet carrier, and the size and specifications of the carrier can be important too. To be safe, choose one that she can sit upright in, stand up and turn around in, and lie inside comfortably without touching the sides. The inside should be padded and water-repellent and have mesh ventilation on at least two sides.

Traveling by car

Of course your Yorkie would love nothing more than to stand on the front passenger seat of your car, stick her head out the window and feel the wind in her face, but this is not the time for free play. She needs to be restrained so she can't distract you while you're driving, or injure you or herself if you have to stop quickly. The restraint is also there to keep your insurance valid if you were to be in an accident.

Ideally you should invest in a certified canine car seat, sized for Toy breeds and with a buckle or clip inside. A booster seat that raises her up is a good choice because it gives her a better view of the world out the window, while also helping to prevent car sickness.

Another consideration is her position in the car. You might love to have her next to you in the passenger seat but, just as with babies, this is not the safest place for her. Only put her next to you, or the driver, if you can turn the air bag setting to 'Off', and push the seat far back. The best place for her is behind and diagonally opposite you, so she can see you to the one side and look out the window to the other.

It's less usual for Toy dogs to travel in the space behind the back seats, like many of the bigger breeds, but if that is your choice, you will need a travel crate or cage. This could be the one you'll be using for other forms of transport, or you might choose her something with a bit more room while still being small enough to fit in the back area of your car.

Do

- For everyone's safety, keep her restrained.
- If she's in a car seat, always attach her by her harness, never a collar.
- Whenever you are lifting her into or out of the car, make sure it is from the pavement side of the road, and never the side with the traffic.

- For her own safety, teach her to 'Stay!' in the car until you lift her out.
- On long journeys, stop regularly for toilet breaks and to let her stretch her legs. These stops will also ease any car sickness she might experience.
- Always keep the car at a comfortable temperature. She should never be too cold or too hot.

Never

- allow her on your lap while you're driving. She must always be restrained.
- put her car seat on the front passenger seat if an airbag is fitted.
- travel with her strapped into a position that is, or will be, in blaring sunlight. If you are driving with the sun predominantly on one side of the car, move her seat to the protected side.
- leave her unattended in a hot or even warm car. Not even for a few minutes. Dog fatalities from heatstroke in cars are frighteningly common and Yorkies are particularly vulnerable.

26. PUPPY-PEOPLE TRANSLATOR

A dog understands your
every word, or so it's said.
The point is, your choice of words is very important.
Even more important though is how you say them. Be
clear in your speech and body language and be gentle
but firm, patient, loving, encouraging, reassuring.

It is also said that a dog can say more with her tail in
just a few seconds than her owner can say in hours. If
she's already in your life, you will be familiar with her
favorite expressions: 'I am so happy to see you!' and
'You are the best thing that ever happened to me!' In her
earliest days with you, you will no doubt have braced
yourself for, 'Your face is like a lovely lolly!' And before
long – but only if you've been 'good' – you could be
surprised by another frequent favorite: 'Your training is
coming along very nicely!'

Yup, a lot of your puppy's body language is really
easy to read, but truth be told the signs are not always
straightforward. How good are you really at
understanding her language and feelings? By way of
example, a wagging tail can be a sign of happiness as
well as one of aggression, so we need to look at the
whole picture including: how she wags it, what the rest
of her body is doing at the time and what else is going
on around her.

To help with this, here are some English-Yorkie translations:

I love you
- Racing to meet you
- Wagging tail
- Licking
- Whimpering

I'm happy and excited
- Tail wagging fast (but watch out as this can also be a sign of concentration or aggression)
- Racing around
- Whimpering
- Pulling lips back and exposing teeth

Let's play
- Wagging tail vigorously
- Rolling head
- Dashing off and jumping back again
- Jumping in front of you, facing you, front legs splayed out
- Elbows on the ground and bottom in the air
- Bounding leaps and running in circles
- Lying down or rolling over
- Barking intermingled with growls (can be confused with aggression)

What is that I hear? Where is it coming from?
- One paw raised
- Head tilted to the side
- Brow raised
- Ears twitch and nose wiggles
- Mouth may be open and panting

Totally chilled out
- Lying on back with legs flopped out
- Curled in a ball
- Lying down watching you

Feeling submissive
- Rolling over onto back, exposing tummy and genitals
- Tail between legs
- Head dipped or tucked in, ears pinned back

I'm curious, and maybe a little concerned, about something going on out there
- Raised paw

I'm frightened or unhappy
- Tail between legs
- Cowering, or lying down
- Ears twitching back and forth
- Staring ahead at object of fear
- Lying down with paws ahead, looking ahead, ready to run
- Raised hackles (hairs along the top of her back)
- Whining or whimpering
- Shivering, trembling or shaking
- Looking to you for help

I'm in pain or frightened and want your help
- Looking from you to whatever it is she needs, and then quickly back again
- Shivering, trembling or shaking
- Whining or whimpering
    This is not manipulation. It's a genuine plea for help. Tell her you're there for her and she can count on you.

Feeling aggressive

- Standing up straight
- Ears pinned back, or sharply forward
- Hackles raised
- Low growl with eyes fixed in a direct stare
- Body tense, ready to attack
- Tail held stiffly, or wagging in stiff, quick, stilted movements
- Barking
- Sudden unpredictable bites

I'm warning you

- Snarling or growling
- Baring fangs

Feeling lonely and locating other dogs, or sending out a warning

- Howling
- Baying

I want your attention: 'hello', 'look at me', 'I'm bored'

- Barking directly at you

I'm begging you. Pleeez!

- Whining, with pleading eyes

    Yes, it's a heart-wrenching expression, but don't give in to that endearing face. Your environment will help you to tell the difference between manipulative begging and 'I'm in pain or frightened and need your help'. If you're eating a juicy sausage that she's hoping you'll share, it's fairly safe to assume she's begging.

27. ADOLESCENCE

Somewhere around six months, your puppy will begin chewing her relentless path to adolescence which is usually the most difficult period for owners. Her newfound independence and low tolerance for boredom will bring an increased interest in exploring, digging, barking and all manner of relationship-testing behavior.

Hopefully the solid foundations you've laid in the early weeks and months will make this phase a little

less wearing. But even with the very best puppy parenting, she will try your patience and you'll need to give her lots of exercise and mental stimulation.

Yorkies' adolescence usually lasts from around six to 18 months – and this is the most likely time for an owner to give up on their dog. Persevere. It's just a stage and it absolutely will get better.

Fear period

As if adolescence isn't tricky enough, around seven to eight months of age your puppy could also experience another fear period, becoming skittish where she was confident before, and scared of many new, and even not-so-new, encounters. If you spot any of these signs you really do need to be especially gentle and understanding.

Sexual maturity

Around six to nine months your puppy will be at the onset of sexual maturity. Your little girl will come into season and be overcome with the urge to roam, and your little boy could begin mounting things and showing aggression towards other male dogs. Both sexes, if un-neutered (meaning they haven't been spayed or castrated) might begin marking their territory by urinating. Basically both sexes will experience hormonal changes that are likely to affect their behavior, so if you're not considering breeding, you will be faced with the important question of neutering.

NEUTERING

To neuter or not to neuter? Although most vets argue in favor of neutering, this is in fact a highly controversial subject, and one that is beyond the parameters of this book. While neutering is likely to reduce bad behaviors, your puppy's health and wellbeing are important factors. Here are some of the key pros and cons to help with your decision.

Advantages of neutering your female dog

(also referred to as spaying or de-sexing)

- It prevents unwanted pregnancies,
- stops her from coming into season (coming into heat), which involves a period of bleeding approximately every six to eight months, for anywhere from two weeks to a month,
- reduces hormone-associated mood swings,
- stops her from trying to escape to find a mate,
- keeps persistent male dogs from pursuing her,
- reduces territory marking by urinating,
- reduces the risk of a number of health problems, including infections of the uterus and ovarian cancer.

Advantages of neutering your male dog

(also referred to as castrating or de-sexing)

- It prevents accidental breeding,
- lessens dominance and aggression,
- cuts back on undesirable sexual behavior, like inappropriate mounting,
- reduces leg lifting and territorial urine marking,
- lowers the urge to run off after females in season,
- minimizes the risk of attack by other males,
- reduces the risk of a number of health problems, including prostate disorders and testicular cancer.

Disadvantages of neutering:

- It involves major surgery,
- can increase the risk of obesity,
- increases the risk of a number of health problems, including bone cancer.

When to neuter

Most Yorkie owners who opt for neutering, have their dogs neutered in their first year. But discuss this with your vet because this is an important consideration, and many studies suggest that neutering too early can result in emotional and behavioral problems.

Neutering won't automatically solve all your puppy issues completely, or overnight, but it should help improve bad behavior in time.

28. GOING FORWARD

So far, this book has focused on the first vital months of caring for a Yorkshire Terrier puppy. Now here are some little but important things to be aware of as she blossoms into adulthood.

Food

By eight months you can gradually start transitioning your puppy on to a 'junior' and then an 'adult' formula, so that around one year old she is on a full 'adult' diet.

Keep to this food as far as possible and practical, because Yorkies often have a delicate digestion, and foods outside their regular diets can cause vomiting or diarrhea.

A very small percentage of Yorkies suffer from food allergies, but if you notice that yours is scratching persistently, rubbing her face, or licking or chewing her tail, legs or paws, it could be a reaction to her diet. The most likely culprits are processed foods containing artificial colors, flavoring or preservatives, followed by seafood, eggs and even certain meats. If symptoms persist, try a food with few or even none of these, adding new ingredients gradually to identify the offending food.

If her food bowls are plastic, try switching to stainless steel or ceramic.

Exercise

From nine months to a year old, when her muscles and bones are more developed, you can start taking her on longer walks if you like, but these should be daily, and not just at weekends. As an adult, she should be getting 45 minutes' to an hour's exercise a day, but if she shows signs of boredom, hyperactivity or starts putting on weight, you can increase this gradually.

Nails

Apart from being uncomfortable, nails that are too long can cause splayed feet and lameness. Some Yorkies never need their nails clipped, but most do. You can tell they need a trim if her toes splay apart, or her nails scratch the ground when she's standing upright. But better still, make this part of her grooming routine, clipping or filing tiny bits at every bath time or trimming session.

If your Yorkie has dewclaws – the nails higher up on the insides of the legs – remember that these need trimming too to prevent them from catching on things or growing into the skin.

Collar

And if she wears a collar, keep up the checks, loosening it whenever it becomes a squeeze to put two fingers between the collar and her neck.

Fine tuning

At a later stage you might choose to improve on your puppy's training, or find that you need help with specific behavioral issues that could've arisen. There are some excellent training guides on the market, or you could seek out a dog behavior expert in your area, but choose one that comes highly recommended.

And if you've got the time and inclination for obedience training classes, she would love you for taking her. They are incredibly enriching for both you and your dog.

29. THERE WILL BE TIMES …

This book is intended as an easy read to offer you some shortcuts with the theory. But there are NO shortcuts with the practice. The practice needs patience and repetition, encouragement and reward.

Yorkies can be too cute for their own good; bossy without strong leadership; determined bordering on stubborn; hyperactive and noisy. But it's these very qualities that make them so priceless. This is why we love them so much. So remember this when you feel your patience running thin.

Tough times

There will be times when your puppy does all sorts of things you don't want her to. She will poop on the carpet; bark when she has something to say; and whine when she's upset or lonely. When she's bored and teething, she will set her little jaws to work on anything she can find, then present you with shredded items of now ex-value.

For months, your house will be littered with toys, and the tick-tack of little paws will be under your feet when you go to the fridge, the toilet, the shower and the front door.

There will be many times when you're at your wits' end and you look at her and think, 'What **have** I got myself into?'

Good times

But you will also have more love than you could ever imagine, and there will be way more times when you think, 'How did I get so lucky?' She will enrich your life with unconditional love and loyalty, energy and courage, and buckets and buckets of laughs.

There will be plenty of times when she is utterly angelic and does all the things you DO want her to do. Praise her with attention, treats, toys – it doesn't matter what – as long as it's something she loves.

Taking-her-for-granted times

And last, but definitely not least, there will be lots of times when she just IS – a calm, quiet presence by your side. Those are the times when it will be easiest for you to forget or ignore her, but those are the times when it is most important of all to remind yourself, and her, just how special she is.

30. USEFUL CONTACTS

American Kennel Club (AKC) – Yorkshire Terriers
www.akc.org/dog-breeds/yorkshire-terrier

AKC Marketplace (Lists puppies available in the
United States from AKC-registered litters)
marketplace.akc.org/puppies/yorkshire-terrier

Animal Health Trust
www.aht.org.uk

Canadian Kennel Club
ckc.ca/en

FCI (Fédération Cynologique Internationale) – The
World Canine Organization
www.fci.be/en

Kennel Union of Southern Africa
www.kusa.co.za

The Kennel Club (UK)
www.thekennelclub.org.uk

The Yorkshire Terrier Club of America
www.theyorkshireterrierclubofamerica.org

The Yorkshire Terrier Club (UK)
www.the-yorkshire-terrier-club.co.uk

INDEX

Made in the USA
Las Vegas, NV
04 October 2022

56550723R00090